Intervention Research

POCKET GUIDES TO
SOCIAL WORK RESEARCH METHODS

Series Editor
Tony Tripodi, DSW
Professor Emeritus, Ohio State University

Mark W. Fraser
Jack M. Richman
Maeda J. Galinsky
Steven H. Day

Intervention
Research

Developing Social
Programs

OXFORD
UNIVERSITY PRESS
2009

OXFORD
UNIVERSITY PRESS

Oxford University Press, Inc., publishes works that further
Oxford University's objective of excellence
in research, scholarship, and education.

Oxford New York
Auckland Cape Town Dar es Salaam Hong Kong Karachi
Kuala Lumpur Madrid Melbourne Mexico City Nairobi
New Delhi Shanghai Taipei Toronto

With offices in
Argentina Austria Brazil Chile Czech Republic France Greece
Guatemala Hungary Italy Japan Poland Portugal Singapore
South Korea Switzerland Thailand Turkey Ukraine Vietnam

Copyright © 2009 Oxford University Press, Inc.

Published by Oxford University Press, Inc.
198 Madison Avenue, New York, New York 10016
www.oup.com

Oxford is a registered trademark of Oxford University Press.

Library of Congress Cataloging-in-Publication Data

Intervention research: developing social programs / Mark W. Fraser . . . [et al.].
p. cm.
Includes bibliographical references and index.
ISBN 978-0-19-532549-2 (pbk. : alk. paper) 1. Social service—Research.
2. Evaluation research (Social action programs) I. Fraser, Mark w., 1946-
HV11.1574 2009
361.3072—dc22   2008039707

Printed in the United States of America

Acknowledgments

We would like to thank the practitioners, students, and faculty colleagues from whom we continue to learn as we work to promote intervention research and evidence-based practice. Scott Briar, Jack Rothman, and Ed Thomas served as inspirations to us in person and in press. Diane Wyant has been especially helpful in editing chapters, and Sarah Zlotnik provided valuable assistance in reviewing the literature. In addition we are grateful to Traci Wike, who compiled the glossary. Specifically, each of us dedicates this book to the following: Mark to Mary, Alex, and Katy Fraser; Maeda to the memory of her husband David Galinsky and to Dana, Adam, and Michael; Jack to Carol, Alice, and Erica Richman; and Steven to Deborah, Claire, and Elijah Day and to his parents Mary and David Hulett.

Foreword

This book is bound to become a well-thumbed treasure for graduate students and researchers working on research designs and grant proposals. The clarity of the thinking and presentation reminds me of the Campbell and Stanley (1963) classic. Yet, there is much more here. In fact, there is enough to help guide practice researchers—whom Fraser and his colleagues call *intervention researchers* because the ideas also apply to service and policy evaluations—through five critical steps.

The authors have been working on intervention studies for a combined total of more than 100 years and it shows. They have now polished their way down to the essential elements of how to develop and test interventions that can add meaningfully to our capacity to serve. At the same time, they illustrate their framework with a wide range of fresh and informative exemplars from contemporary social work and health research efforts, and they tackle topics that readers have a need-to-know about but have never mastered. These topics include understanding of the challenges of evaluating programs in different locations, correcting (as best possible) for biased samples, and the use of tailoring variables.

No volume even remotely approximates the success of this volume in outlining research processes. This work will, at last, provide a social work intervention research book that rigorously integrates conceptualization, design, and analysis in a longitudinal R&D perspective. Although Shadish, Cook, and Campbell (2002) and Rothman and Thomas (1994) have all contributed some intellectual DNA to this work, it remains profoundly original. *Intervention Research* builds on prior books by explicating a tighter linkage among the conceptualization of the problem, the development of a manualized intervention, the assessment of outcomes and intervention processes, and the dissemination of findings plus program resources.

This is not a statistics book—there is scarcely a Greek symbol—but you will learn a surprising amount about the functions of various statistical methods as you design research. *Intervention Research* provides pithy information about what statistical considerations and options will be available at the end of the study to help guide choices at the beginning of the study. However, the greatest strength of the book is its clarity about how to design a promising intervention and how to refine it until it is worthy of extensive evaluation and dissemination. The authors' discussions of how understanding mechanisms that mediate adverse social conditions and how problem theories create leverage points for intervention development are very edifying. Those who have struggled to integrate psychosocial and developmental research into proposals for improving developmental outcomes will find their burden lifted in these pages.

Through precisely written micro- and macro-level examples—including many that build on their personal experiences implementing and testing interventions—the authors clarify how to use a risk and resilience perspective to identify conditions that can be changed. In short, they describe how to design, deliver, and evaluate interventions that build to effective practice.

The structure of the book follows five steps of intervention development, testing, and dissemination. Embedded in this is a discussion of the four stages of intervention manual development, which is interwoven with the overall intervention research framework. The crisp thinking and prose mean that grasping these processes and their integration is as close to effortless as is possible in any book that holds to such high standards of accuracy. The authors have also added a bonus discussion, which integrates the lessons from intervention research into the discussion of *evidence-based practice* and how it must also be informed by factors that are considered in intervention research.

This book provides more information about developing treatment manuals than I have previously seen in any research or practice textbook. Because the development of these manuals, which allows training to a state of fidelity, is critical to testing practice interventions, this is an unmatched value of this volume. The discussion of adaptation of manuals for cultural, ethnic, developmental, and diagnostic subgroups will even bring comfort to those who firmly believe that evidence-based practices are doomed to petrifaction and cannot be applied in real world settings. The authors richly discuss the balance between adaptation and fidelity. There are too many unique nuggets of insight in this volume to mention them all, but the discussion of alternatives to randomized clinical trials that involve sequential designs is particularly striking.

The texture of discussions in this book is nuanced by decades of field research and teaching by the authors. *Intervention Research* shows the refinement of ideas that comes from intensive discussions across time with practitioners, program administrators, substantive experts, methodologists, and students with varied interests. I expect that readers will enjoy being the beneficiaries of these discussions as much as I have.

Richard P. Barth
Dean and Professor
School of Social Work
University of Maryland
Baltimore, MD
USA

Contents

Intervention Research

1

What Is Intervention Research?

A t the core, making a difference is what social work practice is all about. Whether at the individual, organizational, state, or national level, making a difference usually involves developing and implementing some kind of action strategy. Often too, practice involves optimizing a strategy over time, that is, attempting to improve it.

In social work, public health, psychology, nursing, medicine, and other professions, we select strategies that are thought to be effective based on the best available evidence. These strategies range from clinical techniques, such as developing a new role-play to demonstrate a skill, to complex programs that have garnered support in a series of controlled studies, to policy-level initiatives that may be based on large case studies, expert opinion, or legislative reforms. To be sure, the evidence is often only a partial guide in developing new clinical techniques, programs, and policies. Indeed, strategies often must be adapted to meet the unique needs of the situation, including the social or demographic characteristics that condition problems. Thus, the hallmark of modern social work practice is this very process of identifying, adapting, and implementing what we understand to be the best available strategy for change.

However, suppose that you have an idea for how to develop a new service or revise an existing one. That is, through experience and research, you begin to devise a different practice strategy—an approach that perhaps has no clear evidence base, but one that may improve current services. When you attempt to develop new strategies or enhance existing strategies, you are ready to engage in intervention research.

The purpose of this book is to briefly describe intervention research methods, including the design of new services or programs. Intervention research is challenging, and requires a broad array of skills and knowledge. When engaged in intervention research, you not only have to be an expert in the problem area, but you also have to understand the real world of practice; that is, the conditions that affect the provision of a service in various settings (e.g., health centers, schools, hospitals, agencies, organizations, communities). Like an artist or an engineer, you have to lay out the task and enjoy creating solutions. Intervention research takes place at the confluence of imagination, innovation, and science.

This book describes the process of doing intervention research. It is intended for students, practitioners, and researchers who are interested in developing and testing new interventions. The design and development of an intervention is what distinguishes intervention research from evaluation research. Evaluation focuses on assessing the processes and outcomes related to an existing service or program (Rossi, Lipsey, and Freeman 2003). Although intervention research includes evaluation methods, it also entails the formulation and revision of a service or program (Rothman and Thomas 1994). Intervention research involves creative as well as evaluative processes, and it often results in two products: a detailed description of a new program or service and an evaluation of the effectiveness of that program or service.

Intervention research is a dynamic process that involves researchers, agencies, and practitioners. This book is premised on the idea that practitioners and most agencies do not have sufficient time and resources to conduct intervention research. It is through collaboration with researchers, whose work settings vary from universities to research firms to evaluation units embedded in state government, that new interventions are designed and developed. In describing intervention research, we are particularly mindful of the need to fund research activities. Although clinical techniques can sometimes be developed and tested without large grants, the careful, painstaking processes required in intervention projects typically require significant state, federal, or foundation funding. Thus, the process we describe in subsequent chapters guides not only the development of interventions but also provides sufficient detail for developing research proposals.

Defining Interventions

Interventions Are Intentional Change Strategies

As purposeful actions, interventions may operate at the individual, family, organizational (e.g., school), neighborhood, regional, national, or other level. Interventions may be comprised of a single action or a cluster of actions (Midgley 2006). Laws that require children to wear bicycle helmets are singular interventions designed to reduce fatalities and serious injuries related to bicycle accidents. Protective supervision in child welfare is a clustering of interventions designed to ensure the safety of a vulnerable child. Both are examples of intentional change strategies, but one is a focused, narrowly defined strategy, whereas the other is a broad approach involving a variety of agents and actions.

Admittedly, even a focused intervention may require a set of complex substrategies. For example, implementing a bicycle helmet law may require a cluster of activities including educating parents, teachers, and children about the importance and benefits of helmets; certifying that helmets are manufactured at adequately protective standards; ensuring that helmets fit children correctly; and working to ensure that helmets are affordable and available for all families. Furthermore, it would be helpful if practitioners worked with communities and law enforcement agencies to encourage the enforcement of bicycle helmet laws. Thus, even narrowly focused interventions can evolve into complex undertakings in implementation.

In social work, interventions are usually intended to reduce social or health problems. For example, when a social worker uses motivational interviewing to engage a drug-abusing adolescent in treatment, the practitioner is using an evidence-based clinical technique as a part of an overall strategy to reduce his or her client's drug involvement (for information on motivational interviewing, see Miller and Rollnick 2002). Motivational interviewing may be thought of as an intervention: it is used intentionally, it is clearly defined, and the social worker follows explicit practice guidelines to ensure that the process is implemented in such a way as to promote a positive outcome.

Often interventions are more complex. Consider the attempt by staff at the Casey Family Program to improve long-term outcomes in foster care. In the Casey Programs (see text box), a manual-based intervention guided the provision of both a basic foster care program and an enhanced set of services to promote child well-being. Casey staff wanted to know whether their program produced significant life course benefits when graduates—adults who as children had been in Casey Families— were compared with graduates of routine foster care in Oregon and Washington.

The Casey Family Programs:
The Effects of Enhanced Foster Care on Long-Term Physical and Mental Health

In the course of a year, nearly 1% of all U.S. children are placed in foster care and more than 500,000 are in care at any one point in time during the year. Overall, the foster care system is a collage of public and private programs sustained by federal, state, foundation, and other funding. As opposed to public foster care programs operated directly by states, private programs often provide enhanced services, and workers tend to have lower caseloads and higher salaries.

Supported by a foundation established by Jim Casey, the co-founder of United Parcel Service, Casey Family Programs (CFP) offered enhanced foster care in Washington, Oregon, and other states (and in 2003 closed some smaller offices, including the Oregon office). Executives commissioned a retrospective comparison of CFP and public foster care outcomes in Washington and Oregon. They were interested in finding out whether adults who had received foster family care services provided by CFP

(continued)

differed on a variety of health outcomes from adults who had received foster family care services provided by the public system.

During the study period, CFP provided a complex intervention to children who had been removed from their homes because of abuse or neglect. The cost of services was some 60% higher than the cost of services provided in public foster care. Approximately 98% of caseworkers held master's degrees (90%, Master of Social Work) and they carried caseloads of 15–17 children. In comparison, less than 43% workers in public foster care in Washington and Oregon held master's degrees (20–23%, MSW) and their caseloads ranged from 25 to 31 children. CFP foster families were provided a $100 per month retainer and a range of modest financial supports, such as funds for youth extracurricular activities, that are not available commonly in public foster care. In addition, children in CFP had opportunities to receive substantial scholarships (partial to full tuition, room, and board if admitted to a vocational training program or college), whereas children in the two public foster care programs were provided no services or support after 18 years of age.

CFP services were frequently reviewed for best practices, and guidelines for practice were recorded in a manual, *Practice Guidelines for Clinical Practice and Case Management.* The use of the manual was linked to a quarterly assessment process during which all CFP children served during the latter two-thirds of the study were assessed using standardized scales such as the Ansell-Casey Life Skills Checklist and the Achenbach Child Behavior Checklist. From these assessments, eight factors were used in case planning: emotional health, family adjustment and other relation-ships, cultural identification, competence and achievement, physical health, educational development, self-sufficiency, and legal involvement. Most of the foster parents were fully involved as partners in the case planning process.

Children entered CFP after the court and state protective services had terminated parental rights and established protective custody. CFP admitted only children who were eligible for long-term placement because of child maltreatment or child behavioral problems and who could be served in a family setting. The principal reason for placement, however, was child abuse or neglect. The Casey Program was not designed for children where the primary reason for placement was severe emotional, physical, or developmental disabilities. The comparison group included children who met admission standards for the CFP but who were denied admission because there were no case openings, and children who met the study criteria but who had never been referred to CFP.

Because the number of children in public placements was far larger than the number of children in CFP placements, a random sample of

(continued)

CFP-eligible children in public placements in Oregon and Washington was drawn for comparison. Using case records and public records (e.g., motor vehicle registrations), about 72% of all graduates (CFP, 71.6%; Oregon public program, 73.7%; Washington public program, 72.7%) were located and interviewed. Program graduates in the sample had left care from 1 to 13 years prior to the follow-up data collection.

After statistical adjustments for non-responses (i.e., graduates who were not interviewed) and for differences between the CFP and public program graduates on pre-foster care characteristics, health and mental health outcomes were compared for 111 CFP graduates (OR, $n = 29$; WA, $n = 82$) and 368 public program graduates (OR, $n = 126$; WA, $n = 242$). CFP graduates had significantly lower 12-month prevalence of ulcers, cardiometabolic conditions (e.g., diabetes, heart disease), major depression, anxiety disorders, and substance abuse disorders. CFP graduates had a higher prevalence of respiratory disorders. There were no significant differences on pain conditions, such as headaches. Suggesting that these differences may be related to enhanced foster care, CFP graduates were in care for 2 more years when compared to public graduates, and yet they had significantly more stable placement experiences (i.e., fewer disruptions). On balance, compared to graduates in public foster care programs, CFP graduates demonstrated significantly better long-term health and mental health outcomes, although the prevalence of disorders among CFP graduates was still markedly higher than that observed in the general population. This implies that even enhanced foster care programs cannot overcome fully the negative effects of child maltreatment.

Sources: Kessler, et al. 2008; Pecora et al. forthcoming. U.S. Department of Health and Human Services 2008.

Risk Processes

As in the Casey Family Programs, interventions may prevent the development of social or health problems by sustaining normative functioning in the face of adversity, such as child maltreatment. In the field of prevention, interventions are designed to interrupt risk processes leading to social and health problems (Hawkins 2006). For example, in delinquency prevention, a social worker might attempt to reduce risk arising from association with delinquent peers—a well-known risk factor for juvenile offending—by providing a mentor for a child or by providing an opportunity for a child to participate in an after-school program with prosocial (as opposed to antisocial) peers. From this perspective, the intervention is intended to disrupt a *deviancy training* process in which an at-risk child associates with delinquent peers, is reinforced for antisocial talk or behavior, and subsequently engages in delinquent acts (for more on the deviancy training perspective, see Gifford-Smith, Dodge, Dishion, and McCord 2005).

Protection and Strengths

Thus, an intervention is purposive action that is intended to alter a behavior, reduce risk, or improve outcomes (Centers for Disease Control and Prevention [CDC], 2007b). Parenthetically, an intervention may reduce risk either by directly lowering vulnerability (e.g., removing neglected children from their homes and placing them in foster homes) or by strengthening protective factors that buffer against risk (e.g., providing a nurse home visiting program to high-risk parents of newborn children). Enhancing protection is a basis for the strengths orientation in social work (Saleebey 2005). In fact, interventions like the Casey Family Program often attempt to do both; that is, they seek to reduce risk exposure while working to strengthen protective factors.

Intervention Level: Individuals Are Nested in Environmental Influences

Interventions or *programs*—the two terms are used interchangeably in this book—may yield outcomes at the individual, family, group, organizational, community, or other systems level. In addition, we may choose to target an intervention at one level while planning to observe a change or positive outcome at another level. For example, family interventions are often intended to change individual behavior, and they achieve this by altering family-level variables such as family communication or support. In the same vein, school interventions may be intended to improve a child's academic performance (the individual level) but focus on altering school-level variables, such as school size, culture, or leadership. Interventions focused on individuals are usually intended to alter individual attitudes, behaviors, or beliefs. But individual-level interventions may also affect other areas such as disability status, consumer satisfaction, quality of life, or—at the organizational level—the unit cost of services. The key idea is that interventions and their intended outcomes are often nested in a hierarchy. Children are nested in families, and families are nested in neighborhoods. We may produce individual-level outcomes by targeting intervention to one or several levels, and by changing both individual factors and environmental conditions.

Structural Interventions and Structural Models

Interventions are occasionally described as structural. Structural interventions tend to affect social structures such as social controls (e.g., laws), opportunities and access, social roles, and social or economic status. In addition, changes in policies may be thought of as structural interventions. For example, new public policies implementing risk assessment in juvenile justice may be intended to provide the court with systematically collected information on all offenders and, as a result, to reduce racial and ethnic disparities in sentencing (Schwalbe, Fraser, and Day 2007). From this perspective, risk assessment is a structural intervention designed to affect the disproportionate confinement of African American, Latino, and other youths.

However, the word *structure* is more frequently used to refer to a pattern among variables. For instance, a structural model for delinquency might show that peer rejection in elementary school is related to association with delinquent peers in middle school, and that association with delinquent peers in middle school is related to offending in high school. Such a model has two risk factors (i.e., peer rejection and association with delinquent peers) and one outcome (i.e., offending). The model portrays a developmental risk structure for offending. We use this idea of structural models in chapter 3 to discuss problem and program theories.

Place-Based Interventions and Collective Processes

Finally, interventions are sometimes described as place based. On balance, place-based interventions emphasize who, where, and how. That is, they focus on a specific group of people who share common space and/

or who subscribe to common goals and values. For example, communities may be geographically defined social units such as neighborhoods. But communities may also be functionally defined social units such as churches, mosques, synagogues, or temples. Schools occasionally are thought of as communities comprised of students, families, teachers, administrators, and other persons who have a common interest in creating an effective educational organization. A school-based intervention is inherently place-based. The term *place* implies *who* and *where*.

However, the term *place* also implies *how*. Place-based interventions tend to focus on collective processes that bind people together. In other words, the behavior of one community member is thought to influence the behavior of other community members. Through bonds of attachment and commitment, communities (like schools) can have collective efficacy in addressing social problems such as the presence of bullies. From this perspective, collective processes explain how people relate to one another and the products of relationships. Social cohesion and informal social control are thought to mediate individual-level outcomes. In addition, place-based interventions attempt to improve individual outcomes by strengthening social, organizational, and other infrastructures (Wagner, Swenson, and Henggeler 2000). Place-based interventions focus on both location and collective processes.

The Effectiveness of Interventions

Whether intended to change individuals, families, groups, schools, communities, organizations, or legal structures (e.g., policies), interventions vary in effectiveness. Some work well while others do not. When an intervention is called *evidence-based*, it means that the intervention has been evaluated using scientific methods, and the cumulative findings from evaluations demonstrate that the intervention is effective in producing a desired outcome. In this context, effectiveness simply means that the program produces positive outcomes when compared to routine or other ethically acceptable approaches. The terms *evidence based*, *proven*, and *effective* all refer to scientific findings showing that an intervention is responsible for producing desirable results. When the evidence is strong, interventions are called effective.

As shown in Figure 1.1, the strength of the evidence supporting an intervention is gauged by the strength of the research designs used in evaluation processes (Petticrew and Roberts 2003; Shaya and Gu 2006). At the top of this hierarchy of evidence sits meta-analyses of randomized controlled trials (RCTs). Meta-analyses compare and contrast findings across studies. Interventions that have been tested in multiple RCTs and found effective in meta-analyses garner the highest level of support. The next level of evidence is defined by positive findings from a few RCTs but by the absence of meta-analytic studies. Lacking RCT support, cohort studies where participants are tracked before and after exposure to an intervention provide modest evidentiary support, especially if adequate baselines and follow-up periods are used and if a comparison cohort is tracked concomitantly with a cohort receiving an intervention. These constitute the next level of evidentiary support. Following this

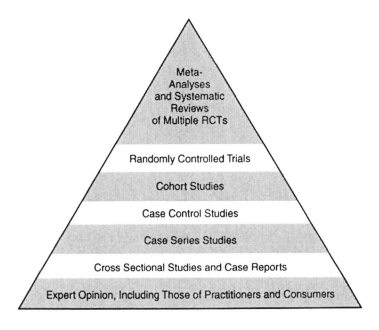

Figure 1.1. Hierarchy of evidence for assessing the effectiveness of interventions.

are case control, case series (multiple case studies), and case anecdotal reports. The lowest level of evidential support is defined by expert opinion, consumer testimony, and practitioner report.

Various professional groups (e.g., American Psychiatric Association, American Psychological Association, Campbell Collaboration, Cochrane Collaboration, RAND Corporation) use this hierarchy and other criteria for designating interventions as effective. These organizations produce lists of evidence-based programs as well as programs that, based on early research, appear promising. The general purpose behind identifying programs based on the strength of their research evidence is to specify which programs have a high probability of making a difference when they are implemented faithfully. For example, see the *What Works Clearinghouse* of the U.S. Department of Education (2007), the Model Programs Web site of the Substance Abuse and Mental Health Service Administration (2007), or the Promising Practices Network of RAND Corporation (2007). It is beyond the scope of this book to compare and contrast the criteria used by these reviewing authorities. Although the criteria vary, intervention research is the basis for these lists, and for concluding that a program is evidence-based.

Intervention research is rooted in scientific methods but it follows a process in which all kinds of evidence are used in the design and development of programs. One might even argue that the hierarchy should be inverted in the early stages of developing a program. That is, the opinions of practitioners, consumers, and experts are sought to identify and sequence relevant program content. And after a program has been formulated, a cohort or case trial with both qualitative and quantitative measures may provide information to refine content or to identify missing content. Only after an intervention has been fully developed would an RCT be considered appropriate. In this sense, the evidentiary hierarchy informs evidence-based practice, but a broad set of methods—both quantitative and qualitative—are used in developing interventions.

Ultimately, intervention research involves the use of scientific methods to show that an intentional change strategy is both *efficacious* and *effective*.

The two words imply different levels of scientific support. Efficacy studies focus on assessing the outcomes of interventions in highly controlled settings; that is, a setting where most alternative explanations can be eliminated so that the researcher can be fairly confident that the intervention was responsible for the observed outcomes. In addition, the researcher, who is usually the developer of the program, has high involvement in every aspect of an efficacy trial. These trials are almost always randomized, which means potential program participants are randomly assigned to either the intervention (treatment group) or to an alternative intervention such as routine services or a support group (control group). The researcher usually provides direct supervision of the delivery of the intervention to make certain that the program is provided in the intended way.

The viewpoint that a program should be shown to have efficacy under ideal conditions before being tested in the real world of practice has dominated thinking in prevention science and at the National Institutes of Health (e.g., Greenwald and Cullen 1985). Indeed, this perspective is so pervasive that two terms have been developed to describe studies: efficacy trials and effectiveness trials.

Although effectiveness trials have a similar level of research rigor, they differ from efficacy trials in that they attempt to implement an intervention *under scale conditions* (Hawkins 2006). In this context, *scale* implies providing the program under real-world practice conditions in which the researchers have limited ability to control implementation factors that might influence the outcome. In addition, an effectiveness trial tests the intervention by providing the program at many sites, and the intervention's developers give researchers at each study site the authority to monitor the provision of services. Thus, the key question in effectiveness trials is whether the positive findings from efficacy trials (i.e., that the intervention produces a desired outcome) can be replicated across many sites without the involvement of the program developer in implementation. Before an intervention is called evidence-based, it should have produced positive outcomes in both efficacy and effectiveness trials.

In establishing criteria distinguishing between efficacy and effectiveness, a committee of the Society for Prevention Research (2007, 1) briefly summarized the difference as follows:

> Efficacy is the extent to which an intervention (technology, treatment, procedure, service, or program) does more good than harm when delivered under optimal conditions. Efficacy is distinguished from effectiveness, which refers to program effects when delivered under more real-world conditions.

Fidelity versus Adaptation: The Source of New Interventions?

As program developers become less involved in the delivery of the intervention, *fidelity* and *adaptation* often loom large as potential concerns. Fidelity refers to the extent to which an intervention is delivered as intended (Sussman, Valente, Rohrbach, Skara, and Pentz 2006). To promote fidelity in efficacy and effectiveness trials, many program developers such as staff at the Casey Family Program create treatment manuals that describe assessment and intervention activities. Treatment manuals are often guided by practice principles (e.g., the Casey Program identified eight factors for use in case planning), and they may include session-by-session protocols for activities, guidelines for group meetings, and worksheets to reinforce or supplement intervention content. When an intervention is highly specified, fidelity refers to "the adherence of actual treatment delivery to the protocol originally developed" (Mowbray, Holter, Teague, and Bybee 2003, 316).

Faithfully replicating evidence-based interventions has become a mantra in social work and other practice-oriented professions. Treatment fidelity is a core idea in evidence-based practice. However, replicating interventions as they were intended turns out to be quite a challenge. For example, broadly implemented smoking prevention programs dramatically reduced tobacco consumption in the United States from 1965 to 2004 (CDC 2007c). But one size did not fit all. As a part of a multitiered prevention effort, alternative smoking cessation strategies were developed for people of different ages and different racial and ethnic backgrounds. Though the same fundamental strategies were used (e.g., motivational interviewing, medications, group work, and skills training), the various programs were tailored to the language, religion, and culture of the target population. "Faithful" replication was based on an understanding of the core elements of effective smoking cessation intervention and a keen awareness that programs must be tailored to the audience's language and culture if they are to have relevance and uptake in the target population.

Indeed, often an intervention has been tested with a particular population, but a practitioner wishes to use it with a different but related population. For example, suppose a family intervention has been shown to be effective with African American families, but a social worker wishes to use the program with Latino families. What could a savvy worker do to adapt the intervention to her cases? First, it is imperative to understand the key features of the intervention. While preserving these features, the social worker might also use her practice knowledge of the population to adapt the intervention to maintain the appropriateness and relevance for Latino families. She could use indigenous Latin concepts like *personalismo* to recruit families or, perhaps, *machismo* to create activities designed to retain fathers in the program. Adaptation refers to modifications made in an intervention when it is applied to a new population. Typically, adaptations are made on the basis of research knowledge plus practice experience.

As one might guess, a dynamic tension exists between adaptation and fidelity. On the one hand, fidelity requires full and faithful implementation without deviation from the design of the original program. The term *program integrity* refers to adherence to the intervention design. We seek program implementation with high integrity. On the other hand, adaptation is recognized as a crucial means for adjusting interventions to the needs and characteristics of clients. After hearing about an extensive adaptation made to the well-supported *Good Behavior Game*, one of the game's developers, Shep Kellam, commented, "That's too bad. You changed the whole dang thing!" His comment raises an important question: Is it possible to both implement with fidelity and adapt to improve the cultural relevance of an intervention?

It is precisely at the intersection of fidelity and adaptation that many new interventions are created. Intervention research is the process of creating and testing change strategies, and these change strategies often arise from adaptations of existing interventions. The greater the adaptation, the greater the responsibility to do intervention research.

Translating Intervention Research Findings into Practice

Once developed, the impact of an intervention is assessed in part by its uptake in practice. However, the factors that influence the adoption of an intervention may be only weakly related to the supporting evidence (e.g., Ringwalt *et al.* 2002). In fact, many evidence-based interventions have scarcely penetrated current social work practice. The need to understand the diffusion of practice innovations has given rise to *translational research*, which is the branch of intervention research that focuses on processes related to the eventual use of a research-supported intervention in practice.

At the distal end of intervention research, translational research is the study of the implementation, dissemination, and diffusion of proven interventions. Those involved in translational research attempt to identify the processes that produce the successful adoption or institutionalization of evidence-based programs. They focus on activities used to integrate an intervention into routine practice. Some interventions, such as motivational interviewing, may be relatively easy to integrate into practice because they do not require extensive training and are highly congruent with current practice. However, other interventions may require the development of new skills or substantial alterations in work routines. For instance, when family preservation services were introduced into child welfare practice in the 1980s, social workers were expected to be available 24 hours a day, but the workplace environment was premised on an 8 a.m. to 5 p.m. workday routine. New flextime policies were needed and, though not formally an element of family preservation, these adjustments to the work environment were crucial to successful program implementation. Translational research focuses on innovations (including organizational structures, such as work hours, and organizational processes, such as professional development and training) needed for the diffusion of an intervention into the service delivery system.

Translational research involves the study of processes related to the acceptance and implementation of proven interventions (Fixsen *et al.* 2005; Glasgow, Vogt, and Boles 1999); however, it does not involve the initial conceptualization and testing of an intervention. It is this conceptualization and testing process that is the central focus of this book. We discuss translation and adaptation as the last step in intervention research.

Intervention Research in Practice

Interventions are change strategies and change strategies can vary substantially in content. Some interventions are *process oriented*—that is, relatively unprescribed—and require the practitioner to make instantaneous decisions about the nature and sequencing of content. In these kinds of interventions, the pace and character of treatment unfold through interaction and social exchange. Some group-based interventions have this dialogical feature, as do many individual and family therapies. Indeed, to some extent, almost all interventions emerge from the dynamic interaction of a change agent with a target population. In this sense, intervention represents an adaptive process that arises from the confluence of a problem or circumstance, a change agent's skill, the content of the intervention, the response of those involved, and the response of the environment.

At the same time, some interventions are *prescribed* (i.e., described in a set of explicit guidelines or steps). These interventions are guided by intervention principles, protocols, or manuals. The *Making Choices* program is one of these comparatively more prescribed interventions. This program has a fully developed treatment manual, and it is our first example of intervention research in social work. Our second example of a social work intervention is the *School Success Profile*, a school-based assessment using a Web-based needs-grid to match children's risk profiles to evidence-based interventions. We describe both programs below and use them as examples of intervention research throughout the book.

The *Making Choices* Program

Background

In the United States, an array of prevention interventions has been developed over the past 20 years. One such intervention, *Making Choices: Social Problem Solving for Children* (Fraser, Nash, Galinsky, and Darwin 2000), was designed to promote social development among elementary school children. By strengthening children's social skills, *Making Choices* was intended to disrupt risk factors associated with poor developmental outcomes in childhood. Fully manualized and delivered by school personnel (i.e., teachers, school counselors, or school social workers), the *Making Choices* program teaches children to purposively regulate emotions, actively solve social problems, and collaboratively engage others in positive behaviors.

The *Making Choices* program is based on social information-processing theory, which is a body of cross-cultural research that specifies the cognitive process through which children encode, interpret, and act on social information (for reviews, see Crick and Dodge 1994, 1996; Dodge 2006; Lemerise and Arsenio 2000). Typically, social information processing involves regulating emotions, encoding social cues in the environment, interpreting the intentions of others (including inferring hostile intent), forming social goals, generating a variety of possible behavioral responses, and then selecting and implementing a response. These aspects of social information processing were used as elements of the *Making Choices* intervention.

A Sequential Experimentation Perspective to Develop Making Choices

The *Making Choices* program was revised using a sequential experimental perspective. Program content was refined iteratively through a series of controlled studies. In the first major study, the initial three program units—about half of the entire *Making Choices* intervention—were pilot tested in a middle school in North Carolina. A sixth-grade cohort was divided into two "schools within schools," and one school adopted *Making Choice* as a part of homeroom coursework. The pilot study included 70 children who participated in *Making Choices*, and 94 children who were assigned to routine coursework. Initial data analyses showed no post-test differences between the experimental and comparison classrooms. However, the research team found a program effect for teacher (classroom) level, and qualitative analyses showed that the students who scored higher on a measure of social information-processing skills had been assigned to classrooms where teachers implemented the program with greater fidelity. In addition, semi-structured interviews with the teachers suggested that earlier intervention was needed. Based on these findings, the age of the target population was lowered to the third grade, and the program was revised significantly (Nash, Fraser, Galinsky, and Kupper 2003).

In the second study, the revised *Making Choices* program was tested with third-grade students. Using a pre- to post-test cluster randomized design, 51 students were randomized by classroom to receive the intervention program and 50 students were randomized by classroom to receive the routine health content control condition. Controlling for pretest scores, children who received the intervention had significantly higher scores on social contact and learning orientation than children in the control condition. Furthermore, the children who received *Making Choices* displayed significantly lower aggression than their peers who received the routine health classes. Important moderation effects (interactions that show differential program effects) surfaced. These indicated the *Making Choices* intervention had had its greatest effect with high-risk children (Smokowski, Fraser, Day, Galinsky, and Bacallao 2004).

In the third study, *Making Choices* was combined with a home-based family intervention, *Strong Families*. Using a wait-list design (which limits inherently the capacity to compare intervention and control groups after treatment), 41 children and their families were randomized to a control group, and 45 children and their families were randomized to an experimental condition (also called the intervention condition). Children in the intervention condition received *Making Choices* while their parents participated in *Strong Families*, which was fully manualized and contained content on parent-child discipline and communication. In contrast to the control group children, the experimental group children demonstrated significant improvements on five of six outcome measures, including ability to regulate emotions, on-task behavior in the classroom, and aggression with peers (Fraser, Day, Galinsky, Hodges, and Smokowski 2004).

Based on these three studies, a fourth study was designed as an effectiveness trial. Three successive cohorts of third graders ($N = 548$) from two schools participated. In 2000–1 school year, children received the routine health curriculum; in 2001–2, students received *Making Choices*; and in 2002–3, children received *Making Choices* supplemented with a teacher involvement protocol and a *Family Nights* program of parent involvement activities. Compared with children in the routine condition, children in both *Making Choices* conditions were rated higher on social competence (including emotional regulation) and lower on post-test social and overt aggression. Moreover, both *Making Choices* groups scored significantly higher on an information-processing skills post-test. Differences on social and overt aggression were maintained six months after the end of the *Making Choices* program (Fraser *et al.* 2005). Analyses showed that information-processing skills mediated both post-test and six-month follow-up differences in overt and social aggression (Fraser *et al.* 2007).

The fifth study in this sequence of experiments was a larger effectiveness trial. Fourteen elementary schools were matched, and within pairs, schools were randomized to receive either routine services or an intervention package comprised of *Making Choices* and teacher training in classroom behavior management. Although findings are not yet available from this study, preliminary analyses suggest that the program has cumulative effects over time. Compared with children in control schools, children in schools receiving *Making Choices* are reported by teachers as significantly less aggressive and more skilled in social relationships (Fraser 2008).

The *School Success Profile*

Background

Based on ecological theory (Bronfenbrenner 1979), the *School Success Profile* (SSP) is a self-report survey intended to measure student perceptions of neighborhood, school, friends, and family (Bowen, Woolley, Richman, and Bowen 2001). For students in the fifth through twelfth grades, the survey consists of multiple-choice questions designed to inform the process by which academic support services and social services are provided in schools. Based on their responses, students receive two summary reports: a Social Environment Profile and an Individual Adaptation Profile. The Social Environment Profile is comprised of 10 dimensions: neighbor support, neighborhood safety, learning climate, teacher support, school safety, peer group acceptance, family togetherness, parent support, parent education support, and school behavior expectations. The Individual Adaptation Profile is comprised of five dimensions: social support use, physical health, school engagement, trouble avoidance, and grades. Taken together, the two profiles provide information for planning individual interventions and, when aggregated across students, data for school and community planning. In this sense, the *School Success Profile* can be viewed as both an assessment that promotes individual provision of services and an organizational intervention that provides information on school-level characteristics and outcomes (see http://schoolsuccessprofile.org).

Scores for the SSP may be interpreted based on national norms (G. Bowen, Rose, and Bowen 2005; N. Bowen, Bowen, and Woolley 2004; Harris and Associates 1997). The *Profile* was designed to provide individual and site-level aggregated reports. After intervention, a retest can provide information on individual change. At the school level, the Summary Group Profile (a composite of Individual Profiles) and the

Detailed Group Profile may be used to identify cross-cutting problems. Information from these two group profiles allows practitioners to identify areas that may warrant group or school-wide interventions (Bowen and Bowen, 1999; Bowen *et al.* 2000; Bowen *et al.* 2005; Nash 2002; Richman, Rosenfeld, and Bowen 1998).

A unique feature of the *School Success Profile* is the expectation that, before results are used, the practitioner will meet with students who completed the survey to discuss findings. This process tends to create a "team" approach, and it promotes data-driven practice. An elementary school version of the survey (*Elementary School Success Profile* [ESSP]) has been developed. It uses a computer-based, engaging format designed for young children, and it has supplemental surveys designed for primary caregivers and teachers (Bowen 2006; Bowen *et al.* 2004). The SSP and ESSP have developed a Web-based resource that allows practitioners to review evidence-based practices (as well as promising practices) that are linked to each of the profile dimensions. Using the Web resource, practitioners can identify areas of concern and review potential research-supported interventions that fit the profiles of the children with whom they are working (see: http://www.schoolsuccessonline.com/clients/sspprograms/default.asp).

Designing and Optimizing Interventions through Research

Both the *School Success Profile* and *Making Choices* were developed from longitudinal research with children, and both programs were refined through a series of studies. *Making Choices* began with literature syntheses on antisocial aggressive behavior in childhood (e.g., Fraser 1996a, 1996b), and the SSP began with reviews of the literature related to school success and drop-out prevention (e.g., Bowen *et al.* 2005; Richman and Bowen 1997; Richman, Bowen, and Woolley 2004). Although rarely discussed, the development of interventions often appears to follow a series of latent steps leading from practice innovations to literature review to pilot tests, efficacy trials, and effectiveness studies.

Indeed, three fundamental activities of conceptualizing, refining, and confirming underlie the design and development of interventions. Leaders in intervention research, Rothman and Thomas (1994) were among the first to chart this process. Extending the earlier work of Greenwald and Cullen (1985) as well as pioneers in intervention and innovation research (e.g., Fairweather, 1980; Havelock 1969, 1995), Rothman and Thomas proposed a six-step model for the design and development of interventions: (1) problem analysis and project planning; (2) information gathering and synthesis; (3) design of the intervention; (4) early development and pilot testing; (5) experimental evaluation and advanced development; and (6) dissemination. In this book, we build on Rothman and Thomas's work, integrating their perspective with the work of others. Throughout, we temper the discussion with our own experiences in developing *Making Choices, Strong Families,* the *School Success Profile,* and other interventions. We focus on optimizing the effectiveness of interventions through conceptualization based on theory and research, refinement during pilot testing, and confirmation in controlled trials. We also expand the emphasis given to the development of treatment or program manuals, showing how problem and program theory can be used in the design process. Finally, throughout the book we use a broad research perspective in which different methods are employed at different points in the design and development process.

Additional Reading

Fraser, Mark W., James K. Nash, Maeda J. Galinsky, and Kathleen E. Darwin. (2000). *Making choices: Social problem-solving skills for children.* Washington, DC: NASW Press.

2

Steps in Intervention Research

Intervention research has three related purposes. First, it is through intervention research that programs are developed and refined. Intervention research provides a systematic process in which research findings, empirically grounded theory, and practice knowledge are conjoined either to create new programs or to modify existing ones. Second, intervention research attempts to answer the fundamental question of whether a program innovation is effective in producing the desired outcomes. Intervention research is crucial in this regard because it employs a range of methods that collectively permit drawing causal conclusions about a program's impact. That is, intervention research allows us to conclude that a program is responsible for an observed outcome and that the outcome is not spuriously the result of some other factor. Third, because intervention research involves drawing these causal inferences, the findings from intervention research can inform theory. Application of findings to theory is often done in post hoc mediational analyses through which the researcher attempts to determine the mechanisms of the intervention—in other words, what made the program work. When the mediators of program outcomes are identified, they can inform broader conceptualizations of social and health problems.

Optimizing an Intervention in a Series of Studies

None of these three purposes can be achieved in a single study. Therefore, a series of studies, each with a different research design, is needed. Suggested by Rothman and Thomas (1994) and others such as Flay (1986), these designs range from small single-case or single-group pilot studies (which carefully chart intervention processes) to more elaborate experimental studies (which assess proximal and distal outcomes). Both inductive and deductive processes are used in an ongoing interplay between data (both qualitative and quantitative) and program design.

It is incorrect to think of intervention research as primarily a quantitative approach relying principally on experimental tests of manualized interventions. Indeed, intervention research may begin with a clinician who, with just one case, tries a new strategy and then writes down what she or he did. Throughout the process of designing and developing interventions, qualitative analyses have an important place. Program materials may be reviewed by consumers or practitioners in focus groups, or they may be critically evaluated by experts in the problem area. Though it obtains little credibility in the hierarchy of evidence (see Chapter 1), this type of review is integral to intervention research. In the spirit of methodological pluralism (i.e., the idea that many methods can inform knowledge development), intervention research nearly always involves a variety of methods. Underpinning all the methods used in intervention research is the idea that program components are optimized in a series of studies conducted systematically and rigorously.

From this series of studies and reviews, interventions often increase in complexity over time. A singular focus may give way to multiple focal points. For example, the *Making Choices* program (see Chapter 1) started as an intervention to strengthen the social information-processing skills of elementary school children, but qualitative data obtained in interviews with teachers suggested that content on emotions and emotional regulation was needed (Nash *et al.* 2003). Identifying this need led to an expansion of the *Making Choices* program. When programs expand to encompass new elements, each new element increases the program's complexity and cost. Each new program element should be tested to ensure that it makes a significant and independent contribution to outcomes.

Although in theory such an approach sounds great, the problem is that it is not possible to test everything. Studies testing competing program elements (also called factors and components) are expensive. Although the process of optimizing an intervention involves sequential experimentation (Collins, Murphy, and Strecher 2007), budget constraints usually allow testing of only the most potentially promising factors (Kazdin 2001).

Think again about the *Making Choices* program. Imagine a scenario in which we wish to test two program elements or factors. Based on the actual development of *Making Choices*, we might test whether the addition of content on emotions produces an added benefit relative to *Making Choices* only (original program) and to routine health content without *Making Choices* (control condition). This scenario yields three intervention conditions: (1) *Making Choices*-Only; (2) *Making Choices*-Plus (program with new content on emotions); and (3) routine health content (a treatment-as-usual [TAU] condition). The second factor we select for testing might be the *change* or *intervention agent*, that is, the person who is responsible for providing the *Making Choices* program. In other words, we want to find out whether the program is best delivered by classroom teachers, school social workers, or school counselors. If *Making Choices* is shown to be effective when delivered by classroom teachers, then the program might be expected to have a broader impact through wide dissemination. This second scenario yields three agent conditions: classroom teacher, school social worker, and school counselor. We can assume that to have minimal statistical power, approximately 30 agents would be needed in each of the nine cells. Whereas finding 90 (30 for *Making Choices*-Only, 30 for *Making Choices*-Plus, 30 for TAU) classroom teachers might not be too difficult, finding 90 school social workers and 90 school counselors would be quite difficult because schools often have only one school social worker or one school counselor. This raises the specter of having to recruit dozens of schools to test whether the intervention agent makes a difference. Although possible, this magnitude of testing would be expensive and difficult to manage.

Therefore, the problem with using a factorial approach to sequential experimentation is that we cannot test all potentially important factors, all potentially important program components, and all the methods of delivery. We must use a partial factorial approach and choose the intervention elements that have the greatest implications. That is, we might select elements that offer promise but may add burden in terms of increased length of service, demand on existing services, or cost. In short, it is important to test whether the promise of greater effectiveness is offset by the burden of greater complexity. When fully implemented in the community, the impact of a program is measured by its *effect size* (i.e., the magnitude of the difference in outcomes between the intervention condition and the control or comparison condition) and its *reach* (i.e., the percentage of the target population that receives the intervention when it is brought to scale). A very effective program that is difficult to implement is likely to have little reach and hence little impact. It is crucial to test program components that, though promising, add further complexity to the delivery of an intervention.

Intervention research is defined, in part, as the process of creating the elements of an intervention and refining those elements in a series of studies. This process is iterative and sequential; that is, the process follows rough steps—though there is disagreement on the number and nature of steps—that allow for conceptualization and recursive reconceptualization. In the end, interventions are optimized within the practical constraints of available resources and current knowledge.

We describe intervention research using a step-by-step approach. However, as suggested previously, the development of an intervention is nuanced by constant critical appraisal based on data, new theory, expert review, and practice experience. Qualitative studies of intervention processes (e.g., extensive interviews and observation of program participants as they go through an intervention) may be useful in sequencing intervention activities or reconfiguring intervention content. New research on the etiology of problems may identify potentially malleable risk factors that should be the focus of new intervention activities or, perhaps, a new element of an intervention. Data from mediation analyses might indicate whether hypothesized change processes produced intended outcomes. If some mediating processes seem more important than others, it may be possible to pare down an intervention and narrow the focus to those processes that appear most likely to produce desirable outcomes. Although we present intervention research as a set of differentiated and sequenced activities, it is the critical interplay of data (especially measurement of program processes and outcomes) with problem and practice expertise that yields over time a refined program with evidence of effectiveness.

Historical Perspective: Intervention Design and Development

As outlined in Chapter 1, Rothman and Thomas (1994) conceptualized intervention research as being comprised of six phased activities. Though there had been many earlier advocates of intervention research as well as other social workers who had written texts on aspects of intervention research (e.g., see Blythe and Tripodi 1989; Briar and Miller 1971; Tripodi and Epstein 1980; Tripodi, Fellin, and Epstein 1978), Rothman and Thomas (1994) were the first to write a methods book on intervention research. Their six-phase perspective on the design of interventions drew on a wide variety of work ranging from anthropology and engineering to the social sciences, and their approach continues to characterize much of today's intervention research. Rothman and Thomas's work is the basis for the five steps in intervention research that we propose later in this chapter. Each phase of the Rothman and Thomas design and development perspective is described below.

Phase 1: Problem Analysis and Project Planning

In Phase 1, a practice-related problem is selected and studied. According to Rothman and Thomas, key activities in this phase are to determine the feasibility of designing an intervention and—if the development of an intervention is considered viable—to prepare a project plan that includes objectives and timelines. During this phase, researchers seek to gain access and cooperation from key informants and agencies, as well as to identify other potential collaborators. Phase 1 centers on developing an understanding of a selected problem from a variety of system-level perspectives and, based on the feasibility of testing a new program in real-world practice settings, establishing a time-specific goal for the development of an intervention. For example, an initiative to reduce falls in assisted living facilities might set program- and policy-level objectives: within three months, develop a system for medications reviews and environmental assessments after every fall episode (program-level objective); within six months, obtain board approval for a test of a medications and environmental screening intervention (policy-level objective).

Phase 2: Information Gathering and Synthesis

In Phase 2, activities center on creating a program innovation as either an addition to an existing program or an entirely new intervention. To avoid replicating someone else's efforts (i.e., developing and testing a program that has already been developed and tested), the researcher needs to conduct an exhaustive review of the literature. In addition, Rothman and Thomas argued that study of success cases complements understanding the causes and correlates of problems, which are often the focus of the literature on etiology and developmental psychopathology. In this sense, the design and development perspective includes the study of resilience, which involves understanding the processes that produce normative behavior in the face of adversity or high risk (Fraser 2004). In the same vein, studying both unsuccessful and successful programs is suggested as useful in identifying potential program components. In engineering, this approach is sometimes called "failure case analysis." That is, when a bridge collapses or a dam fails, engineers try to reconstruct from the rubble what happened and why. Rothman and Thomas argued that much can be learned from understanding program failures and successes.

Phase 3: Design

In Phase 3, the researcher develops the intervention and observational models. A feature of all intervention research is the concurrent development of the intervention and measurement models. The intervention is designed and, at the same time, measures to assess its effects as well as it implementation are adopted. Interventions are often designed to change knowledge, skills, and opportunities. For example, smoking prevention researchers might choose to develop intervention components related to core elements of knowledge, skill, and opportunity such as enhancing knowledge of the long-term health consequences of smoking, increasing skill in refusing a cigarette when offered one, or strengthening laws that regulate the availability of tobacco products. Rothman and Thomas argued that the best outcome measures for interventions are those that are closely tied to the core elements of the intervention. Therefore, in the case of a smoking prevention program, the researcher would develop measures of knowledge, skill, and opportunity that match program components (see, e.g., Prochaska *et al.* 2007). Design and measurement are linked in intervention research: One is not conceived without the other.

The central task during this phase is converting theoretical generalizations—practice implications distilled from the literature—into programmatic prescriptions. We discuss this task in Chapters 3 and 4 as the process of developing program theory and program materials, including treatment manuals. Thorough knowledge of the research literature is the basis for the development of practice-related strategies. In this phase of intervention research, knowledge of the population of interest becomes crucially important. Intervention prescriptions— such as guided dialogue, scripted learning, or group role-play—must be closely tied to theory and research. Finally, in Phase 3, Rothman and Thomas discussed the formulation of procedures for the delivery of an intervention. Today, we might regard this as developing a logic model or specifying a theory of change—topics we address in Chapter 3.

Phase 4: Early Development and Pilot Testing

In Phase 4, an intervention is tested for the first time. Rothman and Thomas (1994) emphasized pilot testing in real-world settings. Programs are usually started in studies that, at least initially, may not have control conditions. In the design and development approach, early development and pilot testing often uses case studies, single-subject designs, and single group pre-test–post-test applications to assess intervention procedures including selection criteria for participants, the training and supervision of intervention agents, and the collection of data. Similar to Rothman and Thomas, our perspective is that early development should focus more on program processes than on program outcomes. For example, in developing an in-home family intervention called *Homebuilders*, Fraser and Haapala (1987–1988) made audio recordings of treatment sessions with 41 families who were referred for child welfare services. Each session recording was transcribed and coded for critical incidents that altered dialogue among family members or changed the course of treatment, and those data were then used to refine the *Homebuilders* treatment model. This sort of qualitative data, when rigorously collected and analyzed, can be combined with data aggregated from single-case or small-group studies to produce useful information that indicates if program processes are operating as intended. Whether conducted as small control-group trials or careful single-group qualitative analyses of program processes, the information from early development and pilot testing is used to identify program content to be optimized in subsequent studies, as well as program implementation issues that must be resolved before moving forward with advanced testing.

Phase 5: Evaluation and Advanced Development

In Phase 5 of Rothman and Thomas's design and development perspective, the emphasis shifts from assessing intervention processes to assessing intervention outcomes. Studies that have assessment of intervention outcomes as a primary goal tend to use a random assignment experimental design. Rothman and Thomas strongly support experimental testing of interventions. In theory, random assignment ensures that the experimental and control conditions are equivalent before introducing the intervention. As a probability-based procedure, random assignment has the advantage of making experimental and control groups equivalent on measured and unmeasured variables when sample sizes are adequate (i.e., randomization requires a large sample). Therefore, differences between groups after the intervention are usually a good—but not infallible—indicator of program effects.

Phase 6: Dissemination

Presuming positive findings in Phase 5, Phase 6 in the Rothman and Thomas model involves dissemination of both research findings and intervention materials. Publication of findings in academic journals is regarded as important because the peer-review process exposes the intervention's design and development activities to useful criticism. Claims of scientific rigor are tested when research reports are reviewed by experts, and the quality of the literature in general is elevated by the exposure of research studies to review by peers.

In distinguishing intervention research from evaluation research, Rothman and Thomas argued that dissemination also involves the creation and publication of user-friendly treatment manuals. Although a relatively recent development, some publishing companies have established book series designed to market treatment manuals, and some professional organizations publish practice guidelines. These new avenues of dissemination reflect the growing importance of evidence-based practice and its reliance on intervention research.

In summary, the design and development approach described by Rothman and Thomas (1994) was a phased procedure for creating interventions. For perhaps the first time in social work, research was conceptualized not as an evaluation project, but rather as a process in which programs were developed successively in steps (see also Onken, Blaine, and Battjes 1997). Whether developed by researchers or arising from innovations made by practitioners, the central concept in the Rothman and Thomas perspective is that there is often a logical process leading from a promising idea to a proven intervention. Following Rothman and Thomas (1994) and others, work on this enterprise of developing interventions has garnered support in agencies, governmental circles, professional organizations, and institutions of higher education.

Emergence of Prescribed Interventions: Manualized Treatment and the Organizational Context

The emergence of intervention research paralleled important advances in practice research. Since the 1970s when—encouraged by funding at the National Institutes of Health—scholars accelerated study of social and health problems, interventions have become more *prescribed* (i.e., carefully described in a set of guidelines or steps). The field is richer today because of the contributions of researchers who developed deep substantive knowledge and became involved in the design of interventions. At the same time, methodological advances in psychometric and statistical analyses have improved our capacity to measure intervention processes and outcomes. In collaboration with practitioners, practice researchers are developing more specified interventions, many of which have been published as manuals.

In essence, treatment manuals are guides for complex tasks (Carroll and Nuro 2001). Manuals specify interventions in bits and pieces, and then sequence these bits and pieces in steps that together constitute a program. For researchers, well-developed, clearly specified manuals are a required part of most federal and foundation proposals. For practitioners, manuals make feasible the replication of evidence-based interventions.

In the next section, we turn to the process of developing interventions, including the development of treatment manuals in an overall design and development process. For this, we draw on Greenwald and Cullen (1985) and on Rothman and Thomas (1994), and we add the work of many other practice scholars to their perspectives.

Steps in Intervention Research

Intervention research involves two somewhat different design processes. As the term implies, the first has to do with research design. Broadly conceived, research design is the systematic process of testing interventions. It is the term we use to describe and organize all the aspects of an evaluation—the sampling and recruitment plan, the number of groups or conditions (e.g., experimental and control groups), the methods of group assignment (e.g., random assignment), the measures used to assess intervention processes and outcomes (e.g., self reports, behavioral observation, parent or teacher ratings), the number of data collection points, and the statistical procedures used to analyze data. In contrast to research design, intervention design focuses on program development. Though analytical in the sense that the research literature is synthesized into practice strategies, designing an intervention involves imaginatively drawing on the literature to create engaging practice content. *Intervention design is the inventive process of identifying and sequencing practice prescriptions.* By prescriptions, we mean all practice activities (e.g., questions for guided group discussion, rules for peer-led confrontation, the storylines of role-plays, and worksheets for homework in a skill-building psychoeducational program) intended to address risk or protective factors and processes. To be effective, these activities must be interesting and relevant; they have to be metered in the context of contemporary issues and language. Effective activities are rooted in understandings, among others, of peer cultures and racial, ethnic, age, and gender differences.

Research and intervention design are technical activities that require expert knowledge and skill. Testing interventions involves knowledge of evaluation methods and, for efficacy and effectiveness studies, skill in experimental design and statistical methods. Designing interventions involves not only substantive expertise in the problem area but also knowledge of the population and the context in which an intervention is likely to be provided. Both the design of interventions and the design of studies involve writing; however, one aspect draws on the parsimony of scientific exposition, whereas the other draws on imagination and literary analogue.

As a sports team may need players who fulfill different roles, intervention research requires the researcher to play many roles. Skills are needed

- to creatively distill prescriptions from research and theory,
- to develop these prescriptions in context-sensitive text,
- to develop an evaluation design with community partners,
- to select or create measures of practice prescriptions, and
- to manage the technical details of data collections and analyses.

This is a tall order. It is why so much intervention research involves teams of researchers and practitioners who bring to the design and development task a range of interests and abilities.

In our experience, the enterprise of intervention research has five steps that unfold over time and across many studies. To be sure, some of the steps include tasks that are themselves sequenced, such as the stages in developing a treatment manual. Further, at each point in the intervention research process, data—both numerical and text—may suggest revision. So reconceptualization and return to an earlier step in design and development activities may be warranted at any time. The five steps of intervention research are to:

1. Specify the problem and develop a program theory;
2. Create and revise program materials;
3. Refine and confirm program components ;
4. Assess effectiveness in a variety of settings and circumstances;
5. Disseminate findings and program materials.

These five steps denote a process for conceptualizing, refining, and confirming the core features of interventions. See Figure 2.1 for detailed description of each of the five steps and for delineation of activities within each step. When processes within a step can be specified as a sequence of actions, we refer to them as stages. The word *stage* is reserved, for example, to describe sequenced activities in creating program manuals. The word *step* is reserved to define the five steps in intervention research. Figure 2.1 is the basis for the content of the remainder of this chapter and of subsequent chapters in the book.

Step 1 of Intervention Research: Specify the Problem and Develop Program Theory

In Step 1, the core features of an intervention are developed. This process involves the detailed description of a problem, a target population, and a change process. The *change process* is sometimes called a *program theory* or, in some cases, a *theory of change* (Fulbright-Anderson, Kubisch, and

STEP 1	STEP 2	STEP 3	STEP 4	STEP 5
Specify the problem and develop a program theory	Create and revise program materials	Refine and confirm program components	Assess effectiveness in a variety of practice settings and circumstances	Disseminate findings and program materials
FEATURES:	**FEATURES:**	**FEATURES:**	**FEATURES:**	**FEATURES:**

Develop a problem theory
• Describe problem in terms of prevalence and incidence
• Develop a structural model, including risk and protective or other factors
• Specify mediating factors and mechanisms
  • Review literature
  • Consult with experts, including practitioners and consumers
	Develop first draft of treatment manual and other related materials	Maintain high control of implementation, test major intervention components separately	Test intervention *under scale conditions* in a variety of settings and circumstances	Publish findings

	Submit materials for external review by experts in problem area and by others with program and population knowledge	Combine intervention components and test in efficacy trial	Estimate effect sizes based on intent to treat	Publish program materials
Develop a program theory • Specify malleable risk factors or mechanisms at various systems levels • Identify intervention level(s), setting(s), and agent(s) • Develop logic model and/or theory of change	Specify essential program content	Estimate effect sizes by moderators	Estimate effect sizes for efficacy subset, i.e., differences in dose/exposure	Develop training protocols and certification program
	Pilot test treatment manual and other program materials	Conduct mediation analyses		
• Specify program inputs • Specify program objectives and activities • Specify program outputs based on mediators • Specify proximal and distal outcomes • Specify a change model • Set benchmarks for success	Expand content of manual to include: • Implementation issues, e.g., organizational and other contextual influences • Training of intervention agents • Supervision of intervention agents • Integration of the intervention with adjunctive interventions • Relation of the intervention to clinical standards, professional guidelines, and evidence-based practice	Test for moderated mediation Develop rules for adaptation based on moderation and mediation analyses		
	Specify preliminary guidelines for adapting content to settings and populations			

Figure 2.1. Steps in intervention research: feature activities by step.

Connell 1998). Program theory delineates both proximal and distal outcomes, plus the intervention process through which the researcher expects to observe positive outcomes.

Problems are often thought of as occurring at the individual level, but they can and should be analyzed from all possible perspectives. In most cases, the first step in understanding a problem involves measuring its incidence and prevalence. It is often possible to use existing data to estimate the prevalence of a problem by social or demographic conditions, such as the percentages of females versus males affected by the problem condition. Prevalence data can be particularly useful in demonstrating risk over time and in identifying high-risk populations.

Thus, as indicated in Figure 2.1, a principal activity within Step 1 involves describing the prevalence of a problem by potential risk groups, whether these groups are defined at the individual, family, group, or organizational level.

After specifying the problem and the population, the research literature is used to develop an understanding of the risk factors that are related to the problem, and the protective factors that may reduce risk. Both sets of factors are important because *it may be possible to reduce risk by strengthening protective factors.* Risk processes can operate at various systems levels. For example, children in a school may have high dropout rates because the school does not systematically conduct assessments and provide supportive services to children with high-risk profiles. Although it might be possible to identify a set of risk factors at the individual level for each child, a preferred intervention in such a school might be at the organizational level, where school policies would be changed to provide for routine assessment and referral. In Step 1, keystone risk factors or processes are identified from a system's perspective.

Building a program theory involves identifying those risk factors that are malleable (i.e., capable of being influenced) in intervention and feasibly changed. Some risk factors are good markers but they are not capable of being influenced or changed. For example, gender is a risk factor for violence because males are more likely to engage in aggressive behavior. However, gender is not malleable. Nonetheless, the way males are raised may contribute to their elevated rates of violence. Thus, although gender itself is not a good candidate variable on which to build program theory, the socialization practices of parents might be targeted for intervention. Specifying a program theory involves identifying malleable risk factors—such as early aggressive behavior in males—and matching the malleable factor to evidence-based change strategies, such as a parenting intervention. In this case, we know that the socialization practices of parents can be changed through psychoeducational interventions (e.g., Fraser *et al.* 2004; Kaminski, Valle, Filene, and Boyle 2008). Parenting skills might be a program component for an intervention designed to prevent violence in males (a nonmalleable risk factor) who demonstrate early antisocial or aggressive behavior (a malleable risk factor in a parenting intervention).

In Step 1, the culminating task is to develop a program theory from a thorough understanding of the problem. Based on a careful review of the research literature and information from practitioners, advocates, experts, and others who know about the problem, the researcher identifies putative risk and protective factors. These factors become the basis for the design of program components and the specification of proximal outcomes (for reviews of the risk and protective factor perspective, see Fraser 2004; Jenson and Fraser 2006). In creating a program theory, the researcher uses evidence to devise a conceptual framework for an intervention. This process involves targeting factors that are feasibly changed through a series of intervention actions or activities. We discuss this perspective in more detail in Chapter 3.

Step 2 of Intervention Research: Create and Revise Program Materials

In Step 2, program materials are developed and then revised based on critical reviews and findings from pilot studies. Indeed, refinement occurs across all the succeeding steps of intervention research. However, the initial task involves fully specifying the intervention and testing it for feasibility. Extending Onken *et al.* (1997), Carroll and Nuro (2001) were among the first to blend evaluation with manual development. Carroll and Nuro's approach traces manual development activities from the generation of rough outlines of promising practices to the design of complex protocols for use with a wide array of populations. Serving as the basis for a more extensive discussion of treatment manuals in Chapter 4, their approach involves three stages.

Stage 1 of Manual Development: Developing a First Draft and Testing It for Feasibility

Stage 1 involves creating a preliminary outline of a treatment plan and pilot testing it for feasibility, which includes assessing the capacity of practitioners to implement and adhere to the proposed treatment plan. In this stage, core components of an intervention are written, reviewed by experts (including practitioners, consumers, and others who have expertise in the problem area), applied in practice, and assessed using a variety of evaluative methods. The theoretical generalizations underlying the intervention should be described in a rationale, and the mechanisms (or active ingredients) through which change is expected to operate should be fully developed. In addition, the duration of the intervention must be determined; usually this is defined by the number of sessions during a given period of time. Session goals and activities are specified as being either essential or optional. The designation of some elements as essential is the basis for developing benchmarks or measures to gauge the fidelity of program implementation.

Stage 2 of Manual Development: Expanding the Manual to Provide Guidance Related to Implementation and Training

In Stage 2 of Carroll and Nuro's program development process, the treatment manual is expanded to include strategies for dealing with common challenges or barriers to implementation. These strategies may encompass adding guidance for managing conflict among group members, ways of retaining reluctant participants (e.g., family members in family treatment), outreach techniques to motivate indifferent participants to engage more fully in activities, and auxiliary interventions to deal with problems such as a client's use of drugs or alcohol before or during sessions. This stage of manual development also involves developing protocols for the selection and training of intervention agents and supervisors. In addition, Stage 2 includes integrating interventions with clinical standards; professional guidelines; and adjunctive programs, treatments, or services (e.g., medications, case management, self-help groups).

Stage 3 of Manual Development: Refining a Tested Manual for Use in a Variety of Settings

Stage 3 activities presume that several efficacy trials have demonstrated that the intervention processes are effective in producing desirable and statistically significant outcomes. In this stage, program materials are tested (a) in diverse populations (e.g., program participants with concurrent mental health disorders such as depression, or concurrent social problems such as homelessness); (b) in alternative practice settings (e.g., delivery of the program in low-income urban areas or in rural communities); and (c) with a variety of intervention agents (e.g., provision of the program by indigenous helpers or by novice versus experienced workers). Here the goal is to fully nuance program mechanisms based on culture, language, and setting. The manual begins to serve as a guide for translating and adapting a proven intervention for dissemination with many different populations.

From Carroll and Nuro's (2001) three-stage process for manual development, it is clear that the design and development of intervention materials take place across all five steps of intervention research. In Chapter 4, we elaborate on a four-stage manual development process and discuss intervention design as a sequence of activities involving program formulation, revision, differentiation, and translation.

Step 3 of Intervention Research: Refine and Confirm Program
Components

Once developed, interventions often have several components, each of which is designed to address important risk factors. In Step 3 of intervention research, these components are tested and refined in studies that maintain high control of program implementation. A variety of designs may be used, and activities should build toward efficacy level analyses in which effect sizes are estimated for each major component or combination of components (Collins *et al.* 2007).

The goal of studies in Step 3 is to identify core intervention components, including synergies and economies that can be realized by combining components. For instance, an intervention may have two major components: one component involves intervention with individuals, and the other involves intervention with the individuals' families. Step 3 calls for a series of studies to be undertaken to estimate the effect of each program component, because one may be substantially more effective than the other, one may be more difficult to implement, or one may be substantially more costly. In this step intervention components continue to be refined and expanded. At the completion of Step 3, the core activities of an intervention or its key components should be well defined and the differential benefits of each component should be clear.

Step 4 of Intervention Research: Assess Effectiveness in a Variety of Practice Settings and Circumstances

Effectiveness trials are designed to confirm intervention components in routine practice. That is, they test an intervention in practice conditions or settings where the researcher may have limited control. Though fidelity is a central aspect of effectiveness trials, the number of sites and participants in Step 4 trials often means that clinical or program supervision is provided by on-site staff. A key feature of effectiveness trials is implementation under routine conditions.

In effectiveness trials, two kinds of dose-related treatment effects are estimated. These estimates are based on intent-to-treat (ITT) and efficacy subset analyses. For ITT, the outcomes of all participants for whom intervention is intended are aggregated—whether they received all, part, or none of the intervention—and compared to the outcomes for persons in a control condition. Efficacy subset analyses focus on estimating the size of the treatment effect for treatment condition participants who are categorized into dosage subsets. From efficacy trials in Step 3, it is usually possible to identify a benchmark of adequate exposure to an intervention. When a subset of participants is selected for analysis because of dosage or exposure level to the treatment, effect sizes can be estimated for *efficacy subsets*, defined as participants grouped by exposure to an intervention. Unfortunately, this type of analysis introduces serious *selection effects* (see Chapter 5), but recent advances in statistical methods provide useful techniques for controlling selection bias. We discuss these methods in Chapter 7.

Step 5 of Intervention Research: Disseminate Findings and Program Materials

A proven intervention is useful only if it reaches the at-risk population, that is, when implemented by agencies as intended and maintained over time.

In its most elegant conceptualization, intervention research should produce programs that, when implemented widely, have a significant impact on social and health problems. From this perspective, it is not sufficient to merely develop and test a program—although this alone is quite demanding. To affect social and health problems, effective programs must be diffused into routine practice.

Dissemination of findings and materials is one aspect of diffusion; however, diffusion is measured more realistically by *practice penetration*, also described as a program's *reach* into a target population or *uptake* by practitioners and agencies. Studies and case examples suggest that programs with a high degree of practice penetration are

- superior to services as usual,
- compatible with agency practices,
- no more complex than existing services,
- easy to try (and reject if they fail), and
- likely to produce tangible results recognizable by authorities as important. (Rogers, 1995)

Rogers (1995) called these conditions *relative advantage, compatibility, complexity, trialability,* and *observability.* To date, no reliable guidelines for dissemination and diffusion have emerged. But clearly, dissemination and diffusion involve creating a wide range of program materials and presenting data in compelling ways to influence public policy makers, agency directors, and other leaders. We discuss the challenge of dissemination and diffusion in Chapter 6.

Conclusion

The purpose of this chapter was to review the historical bases of intervention research in social work and to describe steps in intervention research. We summarized Rothman and Thomas's design and development perspective. Based on the design and development approach, we described our conceptualization of five steps in intervention research: (1) specify the problem and develop a program theory, (2) create and revise program materials, (3) refine and confirm program components, (4) assess effectiveness in a variety of settings and circumstances, and (5) disseminate findings and program materials. These steps focus on optimizing an intervention and its components in a series of studies that make use of a full range of qualitative and quantitative methods.

We emphasize the design, development, and testing of program activities and materials. Although program design begins in Step 1 with the specification of a program theory and reaches a peak in Step 2 with the first draft of a manual, it continues in Step 3 and Step 4 as data are used to undertake increasingly sophisticated refinements that provide for the delivery of an intervention in a variety of practice contexts. In the following chapters, we review each step of this intervention research process and give examples from the development of the *Making Choices* and *School Success Profile* programs.

Additional Reading

Collins, Linda M., Susan A. Murphy, and Victor J. Strecher. (2007). The multiphase optimization strategy (MOST) and the sequential multiple assignment randomized trial (SMART). *American Journal of Preventive Medicine, 32*(5S): S112–S118.

Prochaska, James O., Kerry E. Evers, Janice M. Prochaska, Deborah Van Marter, and Janet L. Johnson. 2007. Efficacy and effectiveness trials: Examples from smoking cessation and bullying prevention. *Journal of Health Psychology, 12*(1): 170–178.

Rothman, Jack, and Edwin J. Thomas, eds. 1994. *Intervention research: Design and development for human services.* New York: Haworth Press.

3

Step 1: Specify the Problem and Develop a Program Theory

Early social researchers were interested in demonstrating whether programs had positive effects on significant social problems such as delinquency, child maltreatment, and drug abuse. They were less interested in showing that programs had positive effects on proximal outcomes such as acquisition of new skills, changes in social support, or compliance with treatment. They tended to focus on long-term outcomes, with emphasis placed on distal effects, and interventions were broadly conceptualized.

Consider an example from the 1941 Cambridge-Somerville Youth Study that was designed to test the effects of case advocacy and supportive guidance on delinquency (Powers, Witmer, and Allport 1951). Using a sample of 431 boys in Massachusetts, the researchers matched the study participants on characteristics including age, physique, family discipline, religion, ethnicity, and neighborhood crime. Within pairs, one boy was randomized to an intervention group and the other to a control group. In the intervention condition, the boys began receiving academic tutoring, medical care, and general mentoring when they were about ten-and-a-half, and these supports continued until they reached age sixteen.

On average, the case workers visited the boys in their homes twice a month, and also took the boys to sporting events and other community activities. In addition, the intervention group boys participated in program-supported camping trips and summer camps. Well intended, the basic idea behind the intervention was to provide friendly, supportive counsel to high-risk boys and their families. Serious crimes were recorded after age seventeen and used as the outcome measure. At the end of the study period, no significant differences were found between the treatment and control group boys (McCord 1992; Powers, Witmer, and Allport 1951). However, findings from a thirty-year follow-up suggested that the boys in the treatment group fared worse in adulthood and reported higher rates of violent crime and alcoholism than the control group boys (Dishion, McCord, and Poulin 1999; McCord 1992). The follow-up study concluded that supportive counseling was not effective, and suggested that aggregating high-risk youth may have a corrupting and deleterious effect (also called deviancy training, see Gifford-Smith *et al.* 2005).

Together with other early studies that focused on distal outcomes (e.g., Berleman, Seaberg, and Steinburn 1972; Glueck and Glueck 1950; Meyer, Borgatta, and Jones 1965), the Cambridge-Somerville study gave rise to a spate of editorials and reviews that were critical of social work, psychology, and other helping professions (e.g., Fischer 1973). These editorials and reviews tended to fuse professional affiliation with particular interventions such as, in the case of the Cambridge-Somerville study, supportive counseling and case advocacy. The ensuing dialogue gave rise to renewed interest in social work research (Briar 1974; Hudson 1982). Many schools of social work started PhD programs with emphases on research, and MSW training became more focused on evaluating practice (Hudson 1978). The development of greater research capability within the profession brought forth rich and impassioned methodological debate on epistemology and methodology (e.g., Harrison, Hudson, and Thyer 1992; Witkin 1991).

Intervention research emerged during this period of professional self-reflection, intellectual turmoil, and methodological criticism. At the core, practitioners and researchers wanted to improve service outcomes and better understand how programs work. Both groups were frustrated with evaluations that seemed to place too little emphasis on understanding the processes operating within interventions. Whether a program was determined to be effective or ineffective, it was usually unclear *why* this was the case. Evaluations that focused exclusively on outcomes came to be known as *black box* research because complex intervention processes could not be untangled. When a program was declared effective, all we knew was that a desirable social or health outcome was produced by the intervention. Although the program seemed to work, the data that were collected did not explain the mechanisms that produced the positive outcomes. The processes of the intervention remained as cryptic as a magic act because the researchers could not see into the black box.

Intervention research emerged with roots in both quantitative and qualitative research methods. The field grew from the desire on the part of social work scholars to develop innovative programs and test them rigorously in controlled trials. It grew also from the desire to better understand why programs worked and, when they failed—as did the Cambridge-Somerville program—why they failed (Fraser 1994; Fraser, Taylor, Jackson, and O'Jack 1991).

With this heritage, intervention research centers both on program outcomes and on hypothesized change processes operating within interventions. To maintain this dual focus, two kinds of conceptualizations underpin the design and development of interventions: *problem theory* and *program theory*. Problem theory has to do with understanding the biopsychosocial processes that produce social and health problems. Typically, this involves considering both individual factors and environmental conditions. Although based on problem theory, program theory has to do with specifying and matching intervention methods to a range of proximal and distal outcomes. This matching process involves clarifying the causal logic of an intervention and describing how the intervention activities are expected to produce significant effects.

This chapter focuses on the twin conceptualizations of problem theory and program theory. In the first section, we discuss the identification of social and health problems and the specification of the risk and protective processes that give rise to problems. This perspective may be used to describe problems occurring at the individual, family, group, organizational, societal, or other levels. The risk and protective perspective is rooted in ecological and systems theories, and draws from the rich literatures of many other disciplines and professions including biology, medicine, nursing, psychology, public health, and sociology. The second section discusses the design of an intervention based on a program theory. Program theories make explicit how an intervention is supposed to function. If a study shows that an intervention is effective, program theory should explain why—it should illuminate the black box.

Developing a Problem Theory

Though micro- to macro-social in character, interventions in social work share a common focus on enhancing human well-being and helping to meet basic human needs (National Association of Social Workers, 2007). Interventions usually center on significant social problems such as hunger, mental illness, family violence, or child maltreatment. However, a problem focus does not mean that we subscribe to a pathology perspective. Indeed, many interventions are comprised of activities designed to strengthen *protective factors*, which are also called assets or strengths. Protective factors operate to disrupt the influence of risk factors (Fraser 2004). For example, having a supportive and involved spouse may promote a patient's recovery from a heart attack or other serious illness. Living in a neighborhood where adults monitor children may reduce gang activity-related injuries. These factors function protectively—they reduce vulnerability in the presence of risk. To design and develop an effective intervention, we must clearly specify the problem and the mechanisms that produce or suppress it. These mechanisms are often combinations of risk and protective factors. It is not uncommon for an intervention to concomitantly build strengths (i.e., promote protection) and reduce risk.

Problem theory is a portrayal of the individual and environmental factors—both risk inducing and risk suppressing (i.e., protective)—that give rise to a problem or that sustain a problem over time. We use problem theory to identify leverage points for intervention. In defining a problem clearly, we are often able to work backward to identify these leverage points, and to discover the risk and protective factors that may be malleable in intervention. Defining the problem is the first step in building the causal logic of an intervention.

What Is the Problem?

Problems are often easier to identify at the individual level. A teenager has no home, and therefore the problem is homelessness. But is homelessness the only problem? What caused the homelessness? If the root cause is mental illness, homelessness may be a manifestation of an untreated serious mental disorder. Perhaps untreated mental disorders should be the stated problem. If the teen was living on the street, does the problem include drug use or prostitution? Does the problem also include HIV exposure or other serious physical ailments? Even at the individual level, problems are usually complicated. Designing an intervention requires making a strategic decision about where to start. In this case, you might pick homelessness as a starting-point. If you can resolve the homelessness (i.e., the problem of the greatest urgency), you may be able to address the other problems.

Problems can and should be conceptualized at a variety of levels. Indeed, individuals and their families are always embedded in larger systems that define the parameters of services and resources. Returning to the example of homelessness, living on the street may be an unintended consequence of federal or state decisions to limit spending on mental health care for low-income families. Or homelessness could be a distal function of private insurer decisions to limit mental health-care coverage for insured families. Alternatively, it may be a function of the inability of local law enforcement to protect a young person from sexual exploitation in her home or, if drug abuse is involved, the dearth of adequate residential drug treatment programs for adolescents. The policy context creates environmental conditions and service resources that relate to the prevalence of social and health problems.

Acknowledging the policy context, we usually begin to design an intervention by estimating the prevalence and incidence of a problem.

Prevalence is the proportion of a population that has a problem at a given point in time. Incidence refers to the proportion of new cases in a population within a defined period. Incidence is usually expressed as a rate, such as the number of new cases in a year divided by the total population. *Incidence* can be thought of as the chance that someone within the population will develop a particular problem within a defined period. In contrast, prevalence is expressed as a simple proportion, that is, the percentage of people within a population who experience a problem.

Prevalence data are often available from federal and state agencies. The Centers for Disease Control and Prevention (CDC) maintains a Youth Risk Behavior Surveillance System that reports national- and state-level prevalences for fighting, victimization, drug use, obesity, and other adolescent problems (CDC 2007d). The CDC also maintains a Behavioral Risk Factor Surveillance System for adults. It collects state-specific information on asthma, diabetes, health-care access, alcohol use, hypertension, obesity, cancer screening, nutrition, physical activity, tobacco use, and other health problems (CDC 2007a). Similarly, crime data are available from the Federal Bureau of Investigation's (FBI) Uniform Crime Reporting system (FBI 2007), and the National Institutes of Health (NIH) publishes prevalence and incidence data on a wide variety of topics, such as suicide and mental illness (e.g., National Institute on Mental Health 2007a, 2007b). These data are useful in describing the dimensions of a problem, including differential risk based on gender, income, race/ethnicity, and sexual orientation. In short, these public data resources may help you make the case for developing a new intervention.

Understanding the dimensions of a problem is the first step in designing an intervention because good prevalence or incidence data provide clues about who experiences the problem. However, demographic data are primarily useful in calling attention to a problem and establishing the need for an intervention. To design an intervention, you need to understand *how* the problem develops, which includes understanding the risk and protective factors that produce the problem as well as the ways risk and protective factors may vary across populations.

Specifying Mediating Mechanisms

Mapping the interaction of risk and protective factors is akin to specifying the mechanisms that mediate social conditions and behavioral or health outcomes. Suppose that you are interested in developing an intervention to improve the social and emotional growth of children from low-income families. In trying to understand the problem (i.e., the social and emotional growth of children in low-income communities), we might develop a framework using the perspective of parenting as a crucial contributor to the growth of children, and poverty as a disorganizing influence on parenting (e.g., Gershoff, Aber, Raver, and Lennon 2007). The following example, in addition to other examples used in this chapter, are drawn from Gershoff and her colleagues (2007), who study the effects of material hardship on child development. A sequential argument, or risk chain, using this perspective might look like:

1. Poverty and material hardship create parental stress
2. Parental stress disorganizes parenting
3. Disorganized parenting affects a child's social and emotional development.

Problem theory requires identifying targets for change by speculating on risk processes that produce social problems. The risk chain above offers many points for intervention. This risk process might be disrupted at any of these points using a variety of programs including those that reduce poverty and material hardship, those aimed at decreasing parental stress or increasing coping skills, or those intended to alter parenting practices. Speculations that underpin putative risk chains, like the one above, are informed by the scientific evidence and theory. When the evidence is strong, these speculations may take the form of hypotheses. Often, we are able to use path charts (see Figure 3.1) to create a graphic representation of the active pathways in a risk chain.

Figure 3.1 shows a structural equation model estimated by Gershoff *et al.* (2007) for the developmental outcomes of U.S. children entering kindergarten. The model includes the elements we outlined

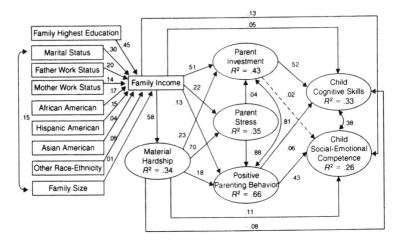

Figure 3.1 Influence of family income and material hardship on child cognitive skills and socioemotional competence. *Source:* Gershoff *et al.* 2007, figure 3. Reprinted with permission.

for the sequential argument and adds a protective factor termed *parent investment.* This term is used to describe the amount of time parents spend with children, parental support for school and extracurricular activities, and, more generally, the academic richness of the home. Notice that in this model, the pathogenic concept of disorganized parenting has been replaced with the alternative *positive parenting behavior,* which is regarded as a strength. As in the Gershoff *et al.* model, conceptual frameworks for social and health problems often contain both risk and protective factors.

To test this model, Gershoff and her colleagues collected data on a nationally representative sample of 21,255 children who entered 944 kindergarten programs in 1998. On the far right side, the figure shows distal developmental outcomes of child cognitive skills (i.e., academic achievement measured through vocabulary, math, reading, and general knowledge tests) and socioemotional competence (i.e., child behavior measured through teacher and parent ratings of the child's social competence, self-regulation, internalizing problems, and externalizing problems). From left to right, the figure specifies the putative risk process, including both risk and protective factors, and shows Gershoff *et al.*'s estimates of the strength of relationships. The numbers associated with each pathway (represented by arrows) range from −1.0 to +1.0. Taken together, these coefficients portray the *structure* of the developmental correlates for child cognitive skills and socioemotional competence; this is one rationale for describing problem theory charts as structural (equation) models.

Using Problem Theory to Build an Intervention

At the start of an intervention research project, problem theory models can be used in two ways. First, prior research may point to pathways leading to a social or health problem of interest. The Gershoff *et al.* model contains two pathways: (1) a parent investment pathway that leads to child cognitive skills, and (2) a parent stress pathway that leads to child socioemotional competence. In the first pathway, academic achievement appears to be influenced largely by a path running from family income to parent investment to child cognitive competence. This pathway is nearly independent of material hardship and parental stress. In the second pathway, child behavior appears to be influenced largely by a path running from family income to material hardship to parent stress to positive parenting to child socioemotional competence. This pathway appears to be independent of parental investment. These pathways specify mediating mechanisms for the effect of family income on the cognitive and socioemotional skills of six-year-old children.

Second, problem theory models identify leverage points. If you were interested in developing a kindergarten intervention to promote cognitive skills and reduce behavior problems, the pathways demonstrated in the Gershoff *et al.* study would give you an evidence base for two intervention strategies. To promote cognitive skills, you might develop a program to strengthen parent investment. Alternatively, to reduce problem behavior (strengthen children's social and emotional skills), you might use these pathways as evidence to reduce material hardship and decrease parental stress. You might also address positive parenting behavior; however, based on the pathways findings, you might not expect positive parenting changes to be sustained unless you also intervene to reduce parental stress and material hardship. By specifying the mediating mechanisms between economic conditions, such as family income, and developmental outcomes, such as child cognitive skills, the research findings from Gershoff *et al.* (2007) provide an evidence base for the design of an intervention.

To be useful in the design of an intervention, mediating mechanisms should include factors that are malleable. On the far left of the Gershoff *et al.* model are factors that contribute to family income, which include sociodemographic characteristics over which we have little control in an intervention (e.g., marital status, education, race/ethnicity, and family size). However, the factors in the middle of the model, such as parental investment, parental stress, and positive parenting behavior, are more easily influenced. Policy- or program-level interventions might affect family income or material hardship by expanding earned income tax credits (e.g., Okwuje and Johnson 2006); by creating individual development accounts or child savings accounts for low-income families (e.g., Schreiner *et al.* 2005); or by providing conditional cash transfers to low-income parents who make investments in the social, cognitive, and health needs of their children (e.g., Maluccio and Flores 2004). Likewise, parental stress might be reduced by organizational-level interventions such as the development of a school-based health clinic that offers positive parenting training among other family services (e.g., Allison *et al.* 2007). Alternatively, parental stress could be addressed through an individual-level intervention such as the creation of a home-based visiting nurse program to provide support to new parents and to teach positive parenting skills (e.g., Olds *et al.* 2007). Structural models anchor program planning by specifying mediating mechanisms that are action points for the design and development of interventions.

Developing a Program Theory

As previously mentioned, the first step in intervention design is the conceptualization of problem theory, which, in turn, forms the basis for a program theory. Described above, problem theory involves understanding the structure of a social or health problem. From an intervention perspective, structural models illuminate the mediating processes, and provide important clues for how and when to intervene. A good problem theory is comprised of mediating constructs that may be changed through program or policy initiatives.

However, problem theories alone are not adequate for planning an intervention because they do not provide enough information. A second kind of conceptualization is needed, which specifies the ways in which the intervention will change the mediating processes: this is called program theory.

Whether implicit or explicit, all interventions have an underlying program theory. A program theory is "the conception of what must be done to bring about the intended social benefits" (Rossi *et al.* 2003, 134). This underlying theory is a portrayal of the causal logic for an intervention. In one picture, a program theory identifies program targets (e.g., parental investment); core activities (e.g., skills training, conditional cash transfers); change or intervention agents (e.g., social workers); and expected outcomes (e.g., academic achievement). Although there are many ways to portray the causal links of an intervention, we describe two frequently used methods: logic models and theories of change.

Logic Models: From Program Inputs to Distal Outcomes

Logic models show the connections between program objectives and inputs and distal outcomes. As Figure 3.2 shows, logic models usually specify an intervention process in terms of core program elements (i.e., objectives, inputs, activities); outputs (i.e., products of program activities); intermediate outcomes (i.e., changes in mediators); and distal outcomes. Inputs are comprised of the resources needed to implement an intervention. These might include staff, training, facilities, and equipment costs such as the purchase of treatment manuals or other program materials.

Logic models are based on problem theory. A core feature of logic models is the specification of malleable mediators (derived from problem theory) as intermediate outcomes. Imagine a scenario in which you are the director of a small neighborhood agency, and you are concerned about poverty and academic achievement. However, you do not have the political capital to influence national public policies that affect the distribution of resources such as family income and material hardship.

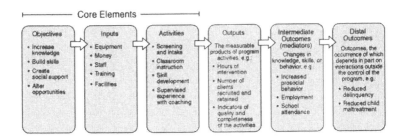

Figure 3.2 Elements of a logic model.

Nonetheless, you want to do something to help parents in your neighborhood. What could you do? Using the Gershoff *et al.* model, you might specify parent investment as an intermediate outcome for a new intervention. The distal outcome for this intervention might be improved child cognitive skills. In this model, you would have to identify program objectives, inputs, and activities to promote parental investment. You would also have to talk about the dependence of parental investment on family income and the ways you might attempt to neutralize this dependence (e.g., providing free magazines, books, and other materials to enrich educational resources in the home).

Program objectives clarify the work focus, and program activities describe specific intervention actions. In logic models, program objectives are constrained to implementation issues rather than distal outcomes. Program objectives usually describe changes in knowledge, skills, attitudes, beliefs, social support, or environmental conditions. These objectives indirectly focus on distal outcomes through the mediators that are identified in problem theory. *If* the mediators are correctly identified in problem theory, *if* program activities truly change the mediators, and *if* the program is fully implemented, *then* distal effects should be observed. That's the logic, but there are a lot of "ifs"—that is, a lot of conditions that have to be met for the distal outcomes to be observed. If the problem theory is wrong, or the change strategies are weak, or the program is poorly implemented, or unforeseen events interfere, then distal outcomes will not be observed.

Clearly, it is important to identify program activities that are potent. In logic models, program objectives are narrowly focused on activities that might change the mediators. Program activities are comprised of action suppositions based on knowledge of what has worked, or produced change, in the past. For this knowledge, you must draw on the research literature. But, although the literature can usually suggest potentially effective program activities, the research may be inadequate as a sole resource. Often, the literature must be supplemented with knowledge derived from practice experience regarding the community or organization, the population, and the problem. Together, program objectives and activities should specify both the nature and amount of the work to be accomplished.

The logic that underpins interventions at any level can usually be distilled from program activities even if the rationale is not explicit in written materials. For example, the 2001 No Child Left Behind Act (P.L. 107-110), which can be thought of as a policy level intervention, was based on a logic model designed to increase academic achievement in the U.S. public education system. Focused principally on the third through eighth grades, No Child Left Behind specified academic achievement as a distal outcome. The legislation created curriculum standards to guide instructional content, and then linked achievement tests to this required content. The Act held schools and teachers accountable for the achievement test scores of their students, and—to ensure that teachers could teach the required content—the Act created minimum qualifications for teacher training and certification (Porter and Polikoff 2007). Broadly speaking, No Child Left Behind represents a standards-based reform strategy (Gamoran 2007). The logic model undergirding the policy is quite simple: (1) change curriculum standards to show teachers what they should be teaching, (2) test the children on required content from curriculum standards, and (3) hold schools and teachers accountable for test scores related to the new content.

The advantage of logic models lies in planning and measurement. From a planning perspective, defining the logic of an intervention requires delineating program inputs, such as resources needed to hire staff or to provide staff training. Specifying a logic model shows explicitly how resources will be deployed to achieve long-term goals. Clearly stating the rationale helps to illuminate the links between program content and program outcomes. From an evaluation perspective, explicitly describing the intervention logic also guides the selection of measures to assess the effect of the intervention. In the case of the No Child Left Behind Act, the logic model suggested that measures would be needed to describe the extent to which curriculum standards were implemented, achievement tests linked to the standards, and schools and teachers held accountable for student test scores. Whether you agree or disagree with a standards-focused change theory, the No Child Left Behind logic model provides a means to measure the success or failure of the legislation.

Theories of Change

Theories of change are closely tied to problem theories and logic models. As an elaboration of logic modeling, theories of change depict a causal chain of activities intended to produce a positive intervention outcome. Theories of change specify models of learning or methods of creating change. From the start to the end of the development of an intervention, a theory of change describes why particular intervention methods were selected. It provides a justification for program activities, and it is explanatory in that it specifies the intervention agents (who), the activities in which they will engage (what), and the setting in which interventions will occur (where). In short, theories of change depict a pathway to intended outcomes. When programs are successful, theories of change indicate why they worked.

Theories of change usually begin with a problem, that is, a problem-related outcome must be specified. A good problem theory is a map describing the conditions, usually risk and protective factors, that produce social or health problems. So, developing a theory of change begins with a long-term goal focused on a problem. Then, drawing from problem theory, malleable intermediate outcomes (mediators) and distal outcomes are identified. These outcomes must be measurable, and benchmarks are often delineated as thresholds for success. For example, assuming from the Gershoff et al. model (2007) that parents' time helping a child with homework is an important aspect of parental investment, then we might select "parental time assisting child with homework" as one intermediate outcome.

Based on prior research or experience, we might say that a program designed to increase academic achievement in a low-income neighborhood will be successful if parents spend five or more hours per week helping their children with school assignments. In part, theories of change are distinguished from logic models by the explicit identification of measures and the selection of intervention benchmarks for success.

Although theories of change are portrayed in many ways, they are usually comprised of components that link constructs from problem theory to an explicit change process. Shown in Figure 3.3, a relatively simple way to present a theory of change is to specify *who* in terms of intervention agents and the target population, *what* in terms of the nature of the intervention activities, and *why* in terms of proximal and distal outcomes. This process yields five core components:

1. Specification of the intervention, including designation of program elements, selection of intervention agents, training of intervention agents, and development of participant screening and recruitment protocols;
2. Implementation of the intervention, including strategies to provide ongoing supervision of intervention agents and to sustain the retention of participants;
3. Response of program participants to the intervention, including the degree of participation in intervention-related activities;
4. Impact on proximal outcomes; and
5. Impact on distal outcomes.

In Figure 3.3, we apply a theory of change model from Snyder *et al.* (2006) to the *Making Choices* program. The goal in this theory of change is to display the importance of clinical skill and training in delivering *Making Choices*. This goal does not diminish the importance of developing a fully specified intervention (a process described in the next chapter). However, in this theory of change, we want to emphasize the linchpin role of implementation, including staff training and clinical supervision, in producing program outcomes. In short, we want to demonstrate that a treatment effect emerges both from specified treatment activities and

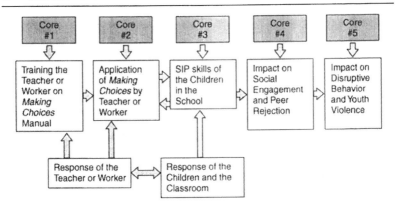

Figure 3.3 Core elements of a theory of change for the *Making Choices* Program.

from spontaneous, dynamic interactions between intervention agents and programs participants.

Theories of change are always accompanied by lots of explanation. Whether for a grant proposal or a project report, change models must be supplemented by explanatory text. Figure 3.3 is a case in point. The figure depicts the core elements of the theory of change in the *Making Choices* program. It shows that beginning with Core 1, the first task in implementing *Making Choices* was the transfer of skills to school-based intervention agents (e.g., teachers, school counselors, school psychologists, school social workers). We argued that this skill acquisition required formal training supplemented by ongoing supervision and support. Core 2 focused on the application of the *Making Choices* protocol. This requires that the intervention agents implement the program as intended. To promote implementation, we scheduled short weekly meetings to review lesson content with practitioners, we provided assistance in tailoring content to meet the needs of students, we made suggestions for adapting content for cultural relevance, and we gave concrete assistance in developing program materials such as game boards and finger puppets. In addition, adjunctive activities that ensure the complete and faithful delivery of an intervention may be described in Core 2. For *Making Choices*, these include referral procedures for students with behavioral needs, on-request consultation from behavioral specialists, and social dynamics training in managing classroom behavior.

Indicated by the two-way arrows in Figure 3.3, dynamic exchanges between students and intervention agents are hypothesized to produce treatment engagement and skill acquisition. Acquisition of social information-processing skills is shown in Core 3 and in the reciprocal causation arrows between Core 2 and Core 3. In showing reciprocal causation, we argue implicitly that outcomes emerge from program activities *plus* difficult-to-specify relational exchanges between intervention agents and children. That is, effects are produced not by a mechanistic, didactic implementation of manualized activities, but rather program effects emerge through learning opportunities derived from program activities, and are mutually created by relational exchanges between skilled intervention agents and children.

As shown in Core 4, producing effects on proximal outcomes is contingent on acquisition of social information-processing skills. In this theory of change, social engagement is hypothesized to be positively related to skill acquisition, and peer rejection is hypothesized to be negatively related to skill acquisition. In logic model fashion, Core 5 displays expected effects on distal outcomes.

Theories of change supplement logic models by addressing practical issues in developing and delivering interventions. In our case, we wished to display the dependence of a well-supported intervention, *Making Choices*, on professional skill in establishing and sustaining learning relationships with children. Similar to logic models, theories of change use constructs from problem theory, which are useful in specifying intervention targets (mediators) and outcomes. Taken together, problem theory, logic models, and theories of change provide conceptual tools for the design of interventions. Collectively, they are used in specifying a program theory.

Conclusion

Program theory explains why and how an intervention will be effective. It portrays the causal argument of an intervention, and it can be expressed in logic models and theories of change. Problem theory is used to identify mediators, proximal outcomes, and distal outcomes. Then a change theory must be adopted. The change theory describes how mediators will be changed. What is your change theory? Is it a standards-based approach like the No Child Left Behind Act? Or does your theory of change use a different approach? The *Making Choices* program relies on a cognitive behavioral model in which children are provided opportunities to learn new skills that problem theory suggests are related to child developmental outcomes. However, *Making Choices* also incorporates key ideas from attachment theory (e.g., effective intervention agents develop bonds of attachment with program participants) and group work (e.g., effective intervention agents have skills in managing large groups such as classrooms).

The design of an intervention is based on two integrated conceptualizations: problem theory and program theory. Problem theory spells out putative risk and protective factors related to a specified problem. It identifies processes that appear to produce or sustain problems. Program theory articulates the logic of an intervention. From the individual level through the policy level, a program theory identifies problem-related processes that may be malleable in intervention. These include processes that may interrupt risk mechanisms by building on strengths and providing protection in the face of adversity. Whether at the individual, family, group, organization, neighborhood, or policy level, program theory specifies the way in which knowledge, skills, support, opportunities, administrative tools, laws, and other strategies are woven together to change conditions that give rise to a problem. Using logic models and theories of change as planning tools, the "nuts and bolts" of interventions emerge in program theory. Program theory is the basis for the development of intervention manuals and protocols, which is the topic of the next chapter.

Additional Reading

Snyder, James, John Reid, Mike Stoolmiller, George Howe, Hendricks Brown, Getachew Dagne, and Wendi Cross. (2006). The role of behavior observation in measurement systems for randomized prevention trials. *Prevention Science*, 7 (1): 43–56.

4

Step 2: Create and Revise Program Materials

Developing the written materials for a program, including treatment manuals, practice protocols, and other resources, is a defining feature of intervention research. Treatment manuals direct interventions by spelling out the specifics of how programs are to be implemented. As such, manuals tend to be prescriptive and many are comprised of session-by-session content.

From program theories developed in Step 1 of intervention research, manuals articulate strategies for changing *malleable mediators*, that is, those factors that seem to explain or account for outcomes and that may be subject to change in intervention. Moreover, manuals are tempered with an understanding of real-world influences that might arise and have the potential to constrain an intervention in practice. These influences include organizational culture and climate, relevant policies, practice guidelines, agency protocols, community conditions, and cultural factors that may affect intervention agents, their training, and program delivery.

Sarah Zlotnik, MSW, MPH, is a co-author of Chapter 4.

Typically, manuals specify program objectives and activities. In some programs (e.g., the Casey Family Program described in Chapter 1), the selection of activities is guided by needs or risk assessment that is used in matching content to program participants. In other programs, a single intervention is implemented. In many manuals, activities and other program content are specified in sessions or lessons, which may include scripted discussion, demonstration, learning exercises, or role-plays. Session materials often contain illustrated handouts to be used in application drills or homework assignments that can be completed between sessions. Some manuals include process tips such as suggested ways for handling interpersonal conflict in group-based interventions. In addition, manuals often contain content on providing services in alternative settings (e.g., schools, after-school programs, neighborhood centers, hospitals, or community clinics), including decision rules to guide the application of content in different kinds of settings.

Step 2 of intervention research is wholly concerned with the creation and revision of program materials, such as treatment manuals. Although manuals are refined across Steps 3, 4, and 5 of the intervention research process, the bulk of the work in manual development occurs in Step 2. In this chapter, we describe the process of developing intervention manuals, and discuss issues involved in the use of written materials in practice. Although we describe the process of manual development as a sequence of activities, manual development is iterative and recursive. Development does not proceed in a steady progression to a final product. It often involves reconceptualization and rewriting. Sometimes, the end product bears little resemblance to the initial drafts.

Variation in Practice Manuals

Typically, manuals are characterized as guides that spell out a program theory and practice content; however, manuals vary significantly in content and length. Some manuals focus on principles or beliefs related to specific models of practice. These kinds of principle-driven interventions tend to leave the content and sequencing of intervention activities to the practitioner. Some manuals are barely more than compilations of suggested activities and only offer lists of resources to be used as need arises. These manuals lack prescriptive clarity and a problem focus. A key feature of a good treatment manual is—in our view—a detailed description of core practice activities and a prescribed course of action (we note exceptions in Chapter 5 where principle-driven manuals, like Multisystemic Treatment, are coupled with extensive training and supervision). Written materials that lack this kind of detailed description are best classified as guides or resources rather than program manuals. Resource guides do not clearly define a program, and thus they leave us vulnerable to the black box conundrum.

To be sure, even detailed manuals differ in the extent to which they are prescriptive. They vary concerning flexibility of implementation (i.e., the degree to which practitioners are encouraged to adapt content); specification of a program theory (e.g., the amount of text allocated to discussion of mediators, logic models, and theories of change); description of techniques (e.g., presentation of sample dialogue that may be used by practitioners); and provision of implementation guidelines (e.g., description of strategies to enhance attendance, decision rules for excluding disruptive clients). Furthermore, manuals differ in terms of the relative importance placed on literature reviews. Some manuals jump quickly to practice objectives and activities, whereas others contain extensive theoretical and conceptual content.

Elements of Treatment Manuals

Both researchers and practitioners broadly and imprecisely use the term *manual*. Manual is sometimes interchanged with other terms that more accurately describe practice tools. For example, the term *curriculum* is frequently used to refer to manuals in which practice activities are psychoeducational in nature and involve didactic processes. A manual may be described as a series of *practice protocols* (standardized procedure guidelines for a specific area of practice), which enumerate steps to reach particular goals, whether general or specific. In addition, manuals are sometimes described as *practice guidelines*; however, our understanding is that practice guidelines are more general decision-making tools based on research evidence and expert practitioner consensus. Practice guidelines aid in the selection of interventions appropriate for a target population and a targeted outcome (Howard and Jenson 1999; Proctor and Rosen 2003). In the literature on evidence-based practice and intervention research, there is no widely accepted definition of the term *manual*. Thus, for the purposes of this text, we define manuals as *guides to practice that describe a problem, a program theory, practice objectives, and program content.*

History of Manualized Interventions

Intervention manuals originally developed as research tools to counteract the black box problem, and they gradually seeped into practice, particularly cognitive-behavioral practice (Addis 1997). Growing out of behavioral and cognitive therapy research, the trend toward manual-based practice emerged in the late 1960s (Luborksy and DeRubeis 1984). An early proponent of manuals, Joseph Wolpe (1969) developed some of the first manualized interventions as part of his work on anxiety-related disorders.

In part, the trend favoring manuals was a response to controversial findings that emerged in the 1950s and 1960s about the ineffectiveness of psychosocial interventions, such as those represented in the Cambridge-Somerville Youth Project. By the late 1970s, research studies had begun to show that therapy was often better than no treatment (Luborsky, Singer, and Luborsky 1975), but intervention processes and outcomes were poorly measured. Too often, interventions were only vaguely described using terms such as casework, in-home treatment, or structural family therapy. This lack of specificity regarding clinical techniques frustrated both researchers and practitioners. The dearth of detailed information was especially frustrating when research findings were positive and there was interest in using programs in community agencies. As a result, researchers began to focus on more clearly delineating therapeutic strategies (Addis 1997).

Efforts grew to specify the components of interventions and to demonstrate the efficacy of specific treatment modalities for clinical problems (e.g., Beck, Rush, Shaw, and Emery 1979). The development of manuals—and indeed intervention research—was fueled by the perspective that a crucial task of practice research was to describe "what works for whom." In addition, other forces have influenced the development of manualized interventions. In particular, legislative reforms have pressed third-party insurers (i.e., programs or organizations that provide reimbursements for health care) to require practitioners to provide interventions with strong evidence bases. In placing a premium on replication of "best practices," these reforms have accelerated the use of manuals.

These developments notwithstanding, the increasing use of manuals in practice has been the subject of considerable debate. Those who favor manual-based intervention cite benefits such as the ability of manuals to help transfer acquired knowledge (Galinsky, Terzian, and Fraser 2006). Proponents argue that manuals increase the quality of services by making it easier to replicate evidence-based services, and they cite manuals as a key vehicle in disseminating best practices (Chambless and Hollon 1998). From this perspective, manuals also contribute to clinical training and supervision, and they facilitate greater consistency in the delivery of services across practitioners with different educational backgrounds (Dobson and Hamilton 2002). In addition, because manuals clarify intervention processes, manuals also strengthen inferences about the outcomes of services (Wilson 1996). Furthermore, manuals increase accountability because they make it possible to monitor the extent to which an implemented intervention is congruous with the written program materials (Luborsky and DeRubeis 1984).

Conversely, criticism of manualized interventions abounds. Generally, objections to manual-based interventions arise from concerns about the complexities of practice, the need for ever-responsive clinical adaptations, and an overall perspective that manuals discount practice experience. Specifically, some critics have argued that manuals try to reduce to a prescribed routine what is essentially an art form (Addis, Wade, and Hatgis 1999). Outside the cognitive behavioral field, practitioners have given manuals a lukewarm reception (Addis and Krasnow 2000; Kendall 1998). Those opposed to manuals hold that the multidimensionality of everyday living situations, organizational processes, and community influences produce complexities that defy manualized treatment (Fonagy 1999). Indeed, the problems confronted by practitioners are often cited as more challenging than those confronted by researchers who test manualized interventions (Abrahamson 1999; Foxhall 2000). For example, practitioners must deal with all clients, whereas researchers often establish sampling criteria to screen out challenging cases, such as those with high comorbidity, those who failed previous interventions, and those with compromised social or environmental supports (Chorpita 2002; Luborsky 1999). Critics note also that manuals can lead to a "cookbook approach," which yields a mechanistic and myopic intervention that devalues practice wisdom and precludes the use of a dynamically changing intervention that is therapeutically reactive to clients' needs (Garfield 1996; Wilson 1996). In addition, opponents of manuals contend that the use of manualized interventions is time-consuming and demands extensive training and ongoing supervision (Najavits, Weiss, Shaw, and Dierberger 2000).

In response to these criticisms, advocates of treatment manuals have acknowledged that using a manualized approach with clients who have multiple problems presents a challenge, but such challenges can be accommodated by most interventions and are not insurmountable (Carroll and Nuro 2002). Well-tested and carefully designed manuals often provide guidelines for varied intervention activities, for the use of adjunctive interventions, and for adaptations determined by client needs (see, e.g., DePanfilis and Dubowitz 2005). Moreover, proponents of manuals have counterargued that if the use of manuals is time-consuming or requires additional training, this may be part of the cost of improving practice outcomes. Advocates have supported this point by noting that most manuals are developed, tested, and refined as part of the process in intervention research. Therefore, manual-based interventions that have produced positive effects in research *should* take time to master because they usually provide a template for doing practice in a different way. Changing practice almost always involves learning new skills, and the investment of time is worthwhile if it improves outcomes.

In our perspective, the crux of this debate is the premium placed on intervention research in which program materials are developed and evaluated systematically. Part of this systematic development includes changes that are made based on data collected during four stages of manual development that are embedded within the steps of intervention research. Described below, each stage of manual development serves a different development purpose, ranging from the initial creation of program materials to the adaptation of materials in different settings. From start to finish in intervention research, manuals are modified based on feedback and critical review—first during formulation, then in revision during pilot tests, next in refinement during efficacy and effectiveness tests, and finally in translation and adaptation for other cultures (e.g., when manuals are extrapolated to new populations). Embedded within intervention research is a design process that involves constant fine-tuning of manuals to improve their fit with current practice and environmental exigencies.

With that said, it is worth noting that it is only when manuals are developed systematically that we can argue with confidence that manual-based interventions improve practice. Not all manuals are based on research. In our view, manual development must be conjoined with research whenever possible, and integrated into a process that involves confirming and refining program components based on the data. When developed in this way, manuals prescribe practice innovations that are likely to improve outcomes.

Stages in Development of Program Manuals and Materials

Intervention research is characterized by interplay between generative processes—used in creating program materials, and evaluative processes—used in estimating the impact of program materials. As noted earlier, interpretative and creative processes are involved in transforming program theory into intervention objectives and content. Often innovative, these processes yield the design of an intervention, including practice activities, materials used for screening and recruitment, and training protocols. In contrast, evaluative processes, which are rooted in the critical traditions of science, provide information on the extent to which programs do what they are intended to do. In intervention research, program formulation and program evaluation are interwoven. The two interact to produce a program of known dimensions and with known outcomes.

Although many conceptualizations of program evaluation can be found (e.g., Rossi *et al.* 2003), few include the development and refinement of the intervention itself. The inclusion of program development is a central feature of intervention research. Figure 4.1 shows the four stages of development of program materials that stretch across the five steps of intervention research. These four stages are: (1) *formulation*, (2) *revision*, (3) *differentiation*, and (4) *translation and adaptation*.

To be sure, the development of program materials can be conceptualized in a variety of ways. In Chapter 2, we described Carroll and Nuro's (2002) three-phase model: (1) developing and testing a first draft, (2) adding content to guide implementation, and (3) refining content for alternative settings. Based on our work and recent advances in translational research, we now propose four stages that further elaborate activities ranging from the initial design of an intervention to its extension to new settings and populations. Because it is literally impossible to test

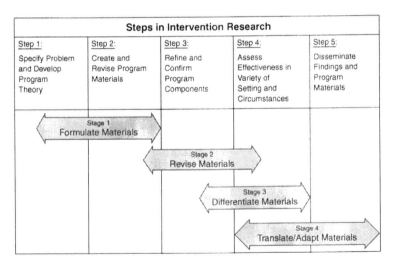

Figure 4.1 Four stages in the development of program materials integrated across the five steps in intervention research.

interventions on every population, we must assume that evidence-based interventions will be used in cultures and settings where they have not been tested. That is, interventions will be extrapolated to populations that appear similar to those in which programs were developed but, nonetheless, for which there are no data regarding program effectiveness. When programs are extrapolated, the essential features of a program are usually preserved. However, at the same time, program content must be translated and adapted to have cultural congruence with the new population. As is demonstrated in Chapter 6, these translational research processes are being given increased attention. In part, evidence-based practice is rooted in the notion that these processes of translation and adaptation will maintain the features of interventions that make them effective while tailoring program content for cultural relevance. This is a tall order, and we address the challenge by proposing four stages in the design and development of program materials.

Each of the four stages is defined by a set of activities that leads to a new set of activities. Shown in Figure 4.1, each stage is integrated with the five steps of intervention research. Although the bulk of program formulation occurs in Step 2 of intervention research (i.e., Create and Revise Program Materials), program objectives and content derive from program theory that is developed as the first step of intervention research. The double-sided arrow for formulation stretches across Steps 1 and 2 to indicate that the foundations for manuals come from the identification of malleable mediators in a program theory. Other stages in the development of program materials are linked to evaluative processes in intervention research. For example, over time and based on data from pilot studies, efficacy trials, and larger effectiveness trials, program materials are refined and then differentiated for various settings and populations. In the sections that follow, the core aspects of the process of developing program materials are described for each stage. The four stages focus exclusively on the development of manuals and other program materials. In contrast, as shown in Figure 2.1, the five steps of intervention research include program design and evaluation processes. Although this chapter focuses on Step 2 of intervention research, it elaborates on the development of program materials by highlighting formulation, revision, differentiation, and translation/adaptation activities that occur across all steps of intervention research.

Stage 1: Formulation of Program Manuals and Materials

Stage 1 in the development of treatment manuals and materials draws on the reading and the research that has been done to Specify the Problem and Develop Program Theory (Step 1 of intervention research). Outlined in Table 4.1, the formulation of program manuals progresses from Description of Problem, to a Program Rationale, to the Program Theory, to a Program Format, and finally to Session Content.

The formulation of a program is founded on a clear specification of a social or health problem, a rationale for intervention, and theory for program development. The latter includes breaking down the problem to identify its context, the factors that give rise to the problem (i.e., risk factors), the factors that suppress the problem (i.e., protective factors), and relevant theories or perspectives that may help to explain the problem (see, e.g., DePanfilis and Dubowitz 2005). These elements are summarized in logic models and theories of change. Taken together, they provide a rationale for a new intervention.

Format of Manual

However, understanding a problem and having a program theory are not enough. They are building blocks. In Stage 1 of manual development, the researcher must select a format for the delivery of the intervention. This format selection involves deciding on intervention content, logically ordering the content, and integrating the content with a delivery mechanism, such as provision by a worker in face-to-face meetings, provision via the Internet in self-paced learning modules, or provision by a classroom teacher as an integrated aspect of a school curriculum. Clearly linked to mediators (i.e., factors that are targeted to bring about change), session or unit content must be developed and sequenced. For some interventions, the researcher will also develop between-session content. This can involve creating homework assignments, application exercises, or interactive projects (e.g., prescribed family outings or discussions). Finally, when

Table 4.1 Stage 1: Formulation of Program Manuals and Materials

Section	Content Areas	Considerations
Description of Problem	• Prevalence and incidence over time • Projections for the future • Prevalence by demographic characteristics • Political and economic costs of the problem • Social significance of the problem	• Who experiences the problem? Is it increasing or expected to increase? How strong are the data? • Do rates vary by race/ethnicity? By gender? By income? By rural/urban? By other factors? • Does the public consider the problem to be important?
Program Rationale	• Existing programs and polices that support the intervention package • Gaps in services • Opportunities for innovation	• What current policies and programs focus on the problem? • Who is at risk of the problem? Why? • Are there new or unrealized opportunities for a program?
Program Theory	• Biopsychosocial and theoretical context for the problem • Risk factors associated with the problem • Protective factors that reduce risk • Structural model of the problem • Specification of mediators • Relevant theories or perspectives from which to understand the problem • Intervention inputs, outputs, and outcomes in logic model • Intervention agents, including pre-requisite knowledge, skill, or experience	• What individual and contextual factors give rise to the problem? • Which of these factors are malleable in intervention? • How might these factors be changed in practice? • Who will provide the program? What contingencies operate on providers, e.g., agency policies or practice standards? • Is the change strategy feasible in the current sociopolitical environment and in real-world practice? Can it work? • What is innovative about the program theory (e.g., targets newly identified mediator, employs new delivery mechanism)?

(Continued)

Table 4.1 Stage 1: Formulation of Program Manuals and Materials (*Continued*)

Section	Content Areas	Considerations

Program Format	• Format of intervention and rationale for format
	  • Prescriptive versus flexibly defined content
	  • Frequency of sessions and duration (i.e., length of treatment)
	  • Session structure and ordering of content
	  • Means for starting and concluding each session (e.g., review of previous or current session content, review of homework, sharing)
	• Nature of between-session activities
	• Guidelines for delivering the intervention, e.g., integration with practice standards, funding mechanisms, best practices
	• Incentives for participation in activities or attendance
	• Provision of environmental supports (e.g., provision of meals, child care, transportation to enhance participation and attendance)
		• Is the intervention targeted toward the individual, family, group, organization, community, or other levels? Why?
		• How often will the intervention be provided?
		• How long will sessions last? How many sessions?
		• Is there a common structure for each session?
		• What is the rationale for ordering the sessions?
		• Is content fully or partially prescribed? What is essential? What can be adapted?
		• Are between session activities (e.g., homework, behavioral charting) specified? For what purpose?
		• How will barriers to participation be addressed?

Session Content	• Objectives and rationale for each session—clear link to program theory • Content and activities for each session • Enrichment or supplemental activities for each session • Review of previous content and preview of upcoming content or activities	• What are the objectives for each session? • Are objectives linked explicitly to mediators? • By session, what content and activities are required or essential? • Either in or between sessions, what activities supplement intervention content?

developing a format and content, the researcher must consider the compatibility with the expected venue in which the program will be implemented. This process involves integrating content with practice standards, agency policies, funding strategies, and other contextual factors that are likely to influence the delivery and, ultimately, the adoption of an intervention. In this sense, we begin to consider dissemination (Step 5 in intervention research) early in the process of program formulation.

Let's take the *Making Choices* intervention as an example. *Making Choices,* a primary prevention intervention for elementary-school children, is based on social information processing (SIP) theory (Fraser *et al.* 2000). The *Making Choices* program is intended to reduce antisocial and aggressive behavior by strengthening children's social skills. As noted earlier, the key mediator is thought to be limited social problem solving skills. SIP theory provides a framework for conceptualizing a social skills intervention. *Making Choices* uses the six steps in the SIP model (Crick and Dodge 1994) as its base and builds on these steps by providing developmentally appropriate activities in six units, each designed to teach one SIP step. In six of the units of *Making Choices,* program theory is explicitly linked to the organizing framework for the intervention and to the skill-building activities within each unit.

The Introduction of the Manual

The introduction to a program manual should spell out the goals of the intervention, the rationale or need, and all the perspectives (theoretical, research, and practice) that inform its use. These perspectives derive from program theory. The intervention goals direct the choice of content and activities for the manual. Tips for using the manual in practice may also be included.

The amount of supporting material in the introduction varies depending on the intended intervention agent and audience. For some, like Heimberg and Becker's (2002) manual for social phobia, the introduction is quite extensive and totals six of the manual's fourteen chapters. In contrast, other manuals may give a short introduction, quickly reviewing the method of delivery, need for the intervention, and frameworks for understanding the problem.

Program Objectives

A detailed description of the intervention process should follow the introduction. To do this, decisions must be made about how the larger purposes of an intervention (e.g., in making choices, acquire social information processing skills) are to be pursued. In other words, how to convert general goals from program theory into action-able objectives (e.g., learn to encode cues), which then guide the development of content (e.g., activities to build skills in identifying cues in the environment). Practice-focused objectives underpin the generative process of creating content included in the manual. Manual authors must determine in what sequence the objectives are pursued and how the objectives may be operationalized through program activities.

Format for Content

It is usually helpful to develop a common format for sessions, including content to be covered through didactic or other means. Keeping the same format from session to session reduces implementation time and promotes uptake by practitioners. In addition, using a standardized format may help the writers ensure that all key intervention components are included in each session, unit, or lesson.

Formats serve different purposes. They organize content across sessions or lessons and are often shaped by the theory of change, (i.e., by the change mechanism through which content is to be learned by program participants). For example, the theory of change may specify how the practitioner and program participants are to be involved in each session, and whether their interaction is through relatively unstructured reflective interaction or through highly structured didactic presentation. More structured interventions are likely to have more complex formats reflecting common program components, such as session-by-session objectives, activities, required resources (e.g., activity worksheets, videos, or other media), discussion questions, recommended reading, enrichment activities, homework assignments, and group interaction strategies.

Let's trace this process by returning to our example from *Making Choices*. The goal of strengthening children's social skills led to the specification of program objectives based on each step in the SIP sequence. Thus, *Making Choices* is divided into six units (plus one introductory unit on emotions). Content in each unit is subdivided into three to six logically sequenced sessions (which we called lessons to mirror the language of the teachers who we hoped would serve as the intervention agents). Each lesson is comprised of activities and exercises to help students master skills related to the unit's focus. Across and within units, lessons use a common format. Each lesson contains objectives, materials needed, review of prior content, and activities. The *Making Choices* manual provides brief guidance on each activity, including potential facilitation questions. Each lesson contains both an opening and closing ritual as well as content that explores the lesson's objectives. In addition, each lesson contains a summary of the main idea and provides potential enrichment activities. Master copies of all worksheets or handouts, which can be easily duplicated for the class members, are also provided.

See Appendix 4.1 for an example of a lesson taken from the *Making Choices* manual (*Unit 4: Goal Formation and Refinement—Setting Social Goals*). This is the first of five lessons that focus on setting relational goals. The lesson begins with a discussion question focused on the idea of social goals, "*What is a goal?*" The content of what defines a goal is explored through two required activities. The first activity is a classroom group discussion to define the core concept of a *goal*. In the second activity, students apply the concept of *setting a goal* to real-world situations. Students are given "Situation Cards" that describe different scenarios, and they are asked to identify potential goals related to each situation. Students share their ideas in a debriefing discussion led by the intervention agent, who might be a teacher, a school counselor, or a school social worker.

Implementation Guidelines or Tips

Manuals often contain cues for implementation. Usually these are down-to-earth tips on how to carry out the activities. Some program manuals provide suggestions about how to involve participants more fully in activities, others include information about group or family dynamics, still others focus on ways to secure community acceptance or to build support with central administrators. Some manuals focus on clinical issues such as strengthening therapeutic relationships. When developing the manual for *Making Choices* (Fraser *et al.* 2000), we chose to include implementation tips in the introduction and throughout the lesson write-ups. The introduction contains background information on group formation and tips on working with groups at different stages of group development. Many *Making Choices* lessons contain *group process tips*. For instance in Unit 1, Lesson 5 on *Recognizing and Managing Feelings*, a tip reminds intervention agents to solicit different ideas for self-talk from group members.

To summarize, during the formulation stage, intervention developers make basic decisions about the goals, objectives, and content. A format is chosen. Content for sessions is written and directions for implementation are developed. Manuals vary in the extent to which they contain complete descriptions of activities, recommended or exemplary dialogue, fully developed worksheets, and, as appropriate, case excerpts or examples to aid in implementation. Nonetheless, the key activity in Stage 1 is, put simply, getting it down in writing.

Stage 2: Revision through Expert Review, Pilot Testing, and Efficacy Trials

As illustrated in Figure 4.1, revision often begins on the heels of formulation. Revision may be based on emerging research, such as new prevalence or incidence information, or on recent data, such as a survey on the public perception of the problem. Sometimes the policy environment changes and produces additional opportunities for intervention. Other times findings are published and suggest new mediating mechanisms. Often, however, revision is a result of expert review of the manual—including reviews by persons knowledgeable about program theory, the practice context, intervention methods, and the population—and pilot testing, which involves the collection of qualitative information from program providers and participants. The findings from expert reviews and pilot studies may suggest content to be added. In addition, reviewers and pilot data may identify content that does not work in practice. They can provide information on the compatibility of an intervention with its intended setting or with adjunctive interventions. Summarized in Table 4.2, revision often involves considering whether the number and sequencing of sessions is optimal, and what are the best ways for intervention agents to deal with implementation issues such as inattention, resistance, conflicts, and comorbidity. Based on evaluative processes that range from review by experts in the field, to single group or case studies, to feedback from controlled studies, revision continues in Step 3 of intervention research, where program components are tested and refined, in Step 4, where an intervention is tested under effectiveness trial conditions, and finally in step 5, where dissemination and diffusion are confronted.

Revision Based on Pilot Testing and Expert Review

Pilot tests of manuals ensure that program content is appropriate for the population and the setting. Similar to expert reviews, a pilot test can indicate that a change is needed in either content or form—or both (Rounsaville, Carroll, and Onken 2001). Suggested above, pilot tests frequently use *mixed methods* (i.e., both qualitative and quantitative methods for data collection) to study intervention processes and to determine whether they are consistent with program theory. Research often focuses on discrepancies or exceptional cases (both failures and successes), where much can be learned about engagement, compliance, and differential response to program content.

To be sure, the term pilot test is used broadly. It encompasses research designs that usually do not have the capacity for causal explanation and, according to the hierarchy of evidence (see Chapter 1), present weaker justifications for effectiveness. These include single case studies and pre-test–post-test trials without control conditions. Pilot tests may involve many of the same activities that are tested more rigorously in Steps 3 and 4 of intervention research, where control conditions are used. These early tests may include feedback from both intervention agents

Table 4.2 Stage 2: Revision of Program Manuals and Related Materials

Section	Content Areas	Considerations
Description of Problem	• New prevalence, incidence, or projection data regarding the problem • New cost information regarding the problem • New data on the social significance of the problem	• Has the prevalence or incidence of the problem changed? • Are new data available on risk populations? • Has the importance or cost of the problem changed? • Has public opinion changed regarding the problem?
Program Rationale	• New programs or policies that affect the distribution of resources or need • New opportunities for innovation	• Is there a new rationale for the program? • Has the risk population or need changed? Why? • Are there new opportunities to provide a program (e.g., a new law or administrative policy)?

Program Theory	• New findings from the literature regarding risk, protective, or other factors, including contextual factors that may condition risk
	• New malleable mediators identified from research
	• From expert reviews, pilot tests, and efficacy trials, refine and confirm program components:
	  – Are program participants correctly targeted and successfully recruited?
	  – Are intervention agents able to provide the program as intended?
	  – Are program participants attending? Who drops out? When? Why?
	  – If attending, are program participants participating as intended in the intervention activities? Do participation rates vary by activity?
	  – What is the effect of the program on outcomes?
	  – Are identified mediators changing as a result of the intervention?
		• Should program components be revised, added, or dropped?
		• Is there new evidence to warrant revising the problem structure, including the specification of malleable mediators?
		• Are intervention agents able to deliver the program as intended? Is additional training or supervision needed?
		• What factors affect organizational readiness for innovation?
		• Are participants from the risk population participating in the program? Are they engaged?
		• From data on dropouts, what strategies could be developed to improve recruitment and retention?
		• What is the impact of the program? What is its effect size?
		• Should the mix of essential versus optional content be changed?

	– Can essential program features be identified in mediation analyses? Is there an optimal mix of program content or components? – Is there an optimal mix of program content or components?	
Program Format	• Dosage and intensity • Participant-related implementation issues: Inattention, resistance, group conflict, low involvement, comorbidity • Organizational and contextual implementation issues, including readiness to innovate or experiment with services, e.g., support from central administration, labor unions, and other stakeholders; compatibility with practice standards, guidelines, and funding mechanisms • Compatibility with other programs and services	• Is the number and sequencing of sessions optimal? • Can common participant-related problems be identified? How should intervention agents deal with inattention, resistance, conflicts, comorbidity, and other implementation issues? • What organizational or contextual constraints affect implementation? • Is the program compatible with adjunctive interventions, such as social support, case management, or medications?
Session Content	• Additions to or revisions of session content based on results from pilot tests and efficacy trials (e.g., if new moderators or mediators were found) • Selection, training, and supervision of intervention agents revised on the basis of pilot tests and efficacy trials	• Is content differentially useful? Should some content be revised or dropped? Should new content be developed? • Is there evidence of drift from the intended intervention? If so, what kinds of training or supervision may be needed

and participants. On balance, pilot tests are designed to describe the process of interaction between the practitioners and participants and, through careful behavioral observation and measurement, to assess the fidelity of an intervention when delivered early in the design and development process. Estimating effectiveness obtains less attention at this stage of program development.

Pilot testing is a crucial aspect of revision. For example, the *Making Choices* program underwent a significant revision based on a pilot test in which qualitative data suggested changing the target population. Pilot testing and expert review are often used during revision to identify program content that warrants modification. Experts, including potential program participants, may review manual content for theoretical application, cultural congruence, setting relevance, and applicability. Review also may focus on the compatibility of program activities with other interventions, such as individual counseling or family meetings, which are in use in the practice setting.

Revision Based on Efficacy Trials

Revision may be based also on efficacy trials that contrast a program with routine services or, occasionally, on trials that compare program components. Discussed in the next chapter, efficacy trials are distinguished by research designs in which random assignment (or an equivalent procedure) is used to assign participants to experimental and control groups. The purpose of efficacy trials is to estimate program effects under optimal conditions with high clinical control—meaning that the program developer frequently supervises the delivery of the intervention and collects both process (e.g., data on program implementation) and outcome information. As noted in Chapter 2, the value of efficacy trials is that they permit drawing inferences about program effects. They are regarded as producing strong evidence of effectiveness. Shown in Table 4.2, process and outcome data are used to address questions related to the efficacy of the intervention: Is the program effective? What is its effect size? Are identified mediators correlated with outcomes? Based on changes in mediators, can essential program components be identified? Should some program components be revised, added, or dropped?

By the time an efficacy trial is being considered, a manual should be fairly complete. It should include detailed descriptions of the problem, a program rationale, the program theory, and session-by-session content. Informed by the pilot data, manuals should also include implementation guidelines and discussion of logistical requirements for the program. These address the context in which the intervention is to be delivered— that is, the primary practice setting for which the program has been developed. In addition, they describe the training and supervision of intervention agents, common problems encountered in the provision of the program, and policies affecting the delivery of services (such as practice guidelines and schedules of reimbursable services under Medicaid).

In revision, an intervention is tested in a primary venue and then, as research advances from refining and confirming program components to assessing effectiveness, the intervention may be expanded to related venues. For example, content for an intervention for children might be developed for neighborhood health clinics, and subsequently expanded to be used in school health-screening programs. During revision (Stage 2) and differentiation (Stage 3) of the development of program materials, the program developers consider the constraints, challenges, and contingencies of various contexts. Emphasis is placed on thoroughly understanding contextual factors in a primary setting. Will the intervention work given the rules and organizational characteristics of agencies? Is it consistent with prevailing practice standards and reimbursement schema? Will activities conflict with other setting-related services or operating procedures? Will changes need to be made in the manual to better tailor the intervention to the socioeconomic status, geographic area, or ethnic background of the target population? Thus, Stage 2 revision focuses both on understanding the primary practice context and improving the "fit" of intervention activities to the contingencies that operate on practitioners and organizations.

Stage 3: Differentiation in the Practice Setting

The activities at Stage 3 of manual development focus on readying program materials for effectiveness studies and revising materials based on the results of both efficacy and effectiveness trials. Shown in Table 4.3, the central theme of differentiation is preparation of program content for alternative populations *in the intended setting*. The assumption is made that the results from trials are positive, suggesting that on average program materials are effective in reducing, preventing, or otherwise producing a beneficial effect on a social problem. Although a manual may have been used with a variety of populations, design and development activities during differentiation focus on adapting content to improve effect sizes (i.e., maximizing the benefit).

To enhance the congruence of program content with the setting, a variety of alternative practice activities are developed in differentiation. After differentiation, manuals may contain a choice of content that can be selected for use depending on the population (e.g., cultural or racial descent); the practice venue (e.g., rural or urban agency auspices); and the intervention agent (e.g., social worker, teacher, or community member). By building on work done in pilot testing and efficacy trials, a fully developed manual becomes nuanced during differentiation on the basis of culture, language, intervention agent, and other factors that may influence outcomes in the intended setting.

Moderated Mediation

Differentiation is often based on data analyses to identify the variation in outcomes that was observed in efficacy and effectiveness trials. These analyses attempt to identify subgroups of program participants who experience significantly different outcomes, whether positive or negative. Statistically, the goal of analysis is to identify moderators and to conduct mediation analyses to test for moderated mediation. By this we mean that analyses attempt to determine whether mediators—specified in program theory—operate equivalently for the range of populations in the primary settings for which an intervention has been developed. For example, we might test to see whether outcomes in *Making Choices* differ for children from Latin and African descent; if they do, we would conduct further analyses to determine whether the social information processing mediators specified in program theory operate in the same way

Table 4.3 Stage 3: Differentiation of Program Manuals and Related Materials

Section	Content Areas	Considerations
Description of Problem	• Differences in prevalence, incidence, and trends across settings, sites, or populations	• Does the problem vary by culture, gender, immigration status, income (poverty), language, race/ethnicity, religion, rural/urban, sexual orientation, or other factors?
Rationale for Differentiation	• Program differentiation by risk group • Program differentiation by agency or setting	• Is there a rationale to modify the program for populations that have different risk exposure? For different kinds of agencies or settings?

Program Theory	• Theory and research suggesting the need to differentiate program content from pilot studies, critical reviews, and efficacy and effectiveness studies, evidence for significant variation (i.e., moderation and moderated mediation) by agency, setting, site, or population
	  – Are outcomes moderated by social or demographic conditions?
	  – Are outcomes moderated by setting, site, agency auspices, or other venue-related characteristics or conditions (e.g., reimbursement policies)?
	  – Which outcomes? Is there evidence for why or how differing outcomes are observed?
	  – Does participation vary by social, demographic, or organizational conditions, including venue-related characteristics or conditions?
		• Does the problem structure, including risk mechanisms, differ across groups with different risk exposure? Is there evidence of moderation and that mediators have different effects for different participants (i.e., moderated mediation)?
		• Are differences sufficiently pronounced so as to warrant the design of a moderator-specific program (e.g., a gender specific intervention)?
		• Are adjunctive interventions needed to support the program (e.g., provision of transportation or food assistance) at different settings or sites or for different populations?
		• Do site and setting (or other venue-related characteristics) make a difference (i.e., does the program operate differentially in different types of agencies, organizations, or settings)? Why? For example, do

(Continued)

Table 4.3	Stage 3: Differentiation of Program Manuals and Related Materials (*Continued*)	
Section	*Content Areas*	*Considerations*
	• Consider effects of organizational and contextual contingencies, including reimbursement schema, best practice standards, labor unions, consumer groups, other stakeholders, and professional guidelines	administrative contingencies, reimbursement schema, or unionization differ by setting or agency? Do these affect the delivery of the program by intervention agents or the support for the intervention by central administration? • Should the program be revised for alternative agencies, sites, or settings?
Program Format	• Dosage and intensity by setting, site, or population • Fidelity across agencies, settings, and sites • Intervention agents from a variety of backgrounds • Administrative support	• Is the number and sequencing of sessions optimal for all agencies, settings, and sites? • How should intervention agents from a wide variety of backgrounds be trained and supervised to provide high fidelity? • What strategies are needed to secure the support of central administrators?
Session Content	• Differentiation of program content for moderators • Differentiation of program content for contextual relevance	• Is content differentially effective? Should content be revised or dropped for alternative settings, sites, or populations? • Should new content be developed (e.g., to promote cultural congruence or gender relevance)?

for Latinos and for African Americans. Then, based on the findings from these analyses, we would adjust the content included in the manual.

It is also possible to differentiate a program based on qualitative data. For example, through intensive interviews or participant observation, researchers might observe variation in outcomes and describe alternative mediation processes. The key idea of differentiation is that a promising program is expanded based on data, either text (qualitative) or numerical (quantitative), which have been systematically collected in a practice setting. Rigorously collected qualitative data can be especially useful in detecting moderated mediation in subsamples that are too small for valid statistical analysis.

What happens if mediation is moderated? That is, what happens if the mediating mechanisms proposed in program theory operate differently for program participants from different racial or ethnic backgrounds, at different risk levels, or in different settings? If moderated mediation is found, program theory cannot be generalized. This is a serious problem. Fortunately, the literature is usually a good guide in program design. Careful program formulation, including specification of a program theory that is based on research with adequate sampling of the risk population, will minimize this problem. But suppose you carefully based your program on the best available information and you still observed moderated mediation.

The answer to this problem is not simple. If the effect of moderation is large and the mediators are clearly different, programs may have to be fully differentiated, that is, developed separately for each population. For example, if gender were to have moderated the outcomes of *Making Choices* and mediators were found to be quite different, one program for boys and a separate program for girls would need to be developed. Given moderated mediation, these programs would operate from different program theories, addressing different mediating mechanisms. However, it is more likely that when moderated mediation is found, program content can be adapted. Activities can be developed and integrated into the intervention so that differences based on moderated mediation are addressed in the course of the intervention.

Often when a program is extended to an entirely new setting or population, differentiation exceeds the bounds of knowledge from previous studies. In other words, the program content is modified and developed for settings or populations not represented in the available data. At this level of program differentiation, activities may involve the translation of manuals into different languages and the adaptation of program activities for different cultures. Translation and adaptation constitute Stage 4 in the design and development of program materials. They are key activities in the dissemination of program findings and materials, which is the fifth and final step in intervention research. As indicated in Figure 4.1, we think of translation/adaptation as overlapping not only with differentiation but also with efficacy and effectiveness trials. In the next section, we describe the translation and adaptation process as a crucial element in the dissemination of evidence-based programs.

Stage 4: Translation and Adaptation

After an intervention has been shown to be effective, it is tempting to assume that it will be adopted by practitioners and the agencies in which they work. But this is a poor assumption. Research shows that many evidence-based programs do not penetrate practice, and, indeed, they languish on the shelves of the researchers who developed them (Fixsen *et al.* 2005; Ringwalt *et al.* 2002). One might ask how can this be?

The answer has many facets. The uptake of programs by practitioners and agencies is affected by contingencies that are partially independent of the base of research evidence. These contingencies include fiscal protocols that, in specifying reimbursement rates for certain kinds of services, do not provide a mechanism to fund newly developed programs. They include agency policies, informal practices, and organizational culture that discourage innovation and experimentation. Occasionally, too, policies place emphasis on one set of outcomes at the expense of other outcomes. For example, in U.S. public schools, the emphasis on testing created by the 2001 No Child Left Behind Act (P.L. 107-110) placed such a premium on classroom instruction in math and reading that many teachers were reluctant to use class time for innovative prevention programs, such as social or character development education (Greenberg 2004).

The answer is rooted also in the nature of intervention research and the kind of program materials required for efficacy and effectiveness trials. Research program materials tend to be sparser than commercially available program materials. At the expense of graphics, layout, readability, and visual appeal, research treatment manuals are often comprised of dense text. Handouts may not be fully refined, and they may require more preparation time than practitioners judge as reasonable or have available. In the same vein, artwork is often more primitive or may not represent the cultural diversity that is required in commercial products. In addition, researchers are typically unable to provide extensive training in the interventions they developed. Researchers often work in universities or institutes that are not well configured to develop commercial training initiatives. Thus, newly developed programs normally do not have an off-the-shelf, user-friendly character, and the researchers who develop programs usually lack the management support to provide training on a widespread basis. Therefore, at the end of the intervention research process, a new set of challenging activities emerges. These activities focus on preparing programs and other materials for dissemination.

Anticipating Dissemination

Dissemination begins early in the design and development process. The translation and adaptation of program materials should begin during efficacy and effectiveness trials. Even as programs are being tested, the program developers must consider whether the targeted problem is widely experienced in a variety of settings, such as rural as well as urban areas or in other countries, and whether mediating mechanisms specified in program theory can be generalized. Core considerations include: To what extent does evidence suggest that program theory is applicable across cultures, settings, and populations? Are program materials culturally congruent across populations? Are standards for implementation and adaptation clear? Indeed, do program materials provide instructions for adaptation? And in a pragmatic sense, what is the cost of program materials and training? Is the program affordable? (see Table 4.4).

Translation and Cultural Adaptation

Inevitably, evidence-based programs will be screened for adoption in cultures quite different from the ones in which they were developed. When this happens, what systematic processes might be followed to guide the translation and cultural adaptation of program materials? We can think about this as the problem of extrapolation. How should evidence-based programs be extrapolated? That is, how should these programs be modified for entirely new practice contexts or populations? Although extrapolations may take place in contexts that are similar to the settings in which interventions were developed, we focus on extending the use of program materials to other countries and cultures, and we illustrate our discussion with reference to our experience with *Making Choices* in the People's Republic of China. We discuss a somewhat broader conceptualization of adaptation in Chapter 6.

Translation and cultural adaptation involve modifying program content to reflect normative beliefs and values in a new target population or setting. After translation, adaptation often leads to respecification of core program constructs in the form of culturally nuanced activities. Though others have described adaptation as a multistep process involving sociopolitical analyses to improve the fit of implementation strategies with the environment (Backer 2002), we propose three steps that focus somewhat more on linguistic and cultural adaptation:

1. Expert review of program theory and materials for cultural and contextual congruence.
2. Translation and back-translation of program materials, with consensual review for idiomatic precision.
3. Cultural adaptation of core constructs and program activities.

Expert Review for Cultural and Contextual Congruence

The first step in translation and adaptation is expert review of the relevance of program theory and content. This review involves assessing the fit of program content to cultural beliefs and practices. It also involves an assessment of the organizational context in which an intervention is to be implemented. When *Making Choices* was adapted for children in China,

Table 4.4 Stage 4: Translation and Adaptation of Program Manuals and Related Materials

Section	Content Areas	Considerations
Description of Problem	• Incidence, prevalence, and trends by implementation domain	• Should the problem be described more globally to extrapolate to all possible settings, sites, and populations where the intervention may be used?
Program Rationale	• Generalization of risk mechanism to populations for which no data were collected • Cross-cultural application of program	• How broadly applicable is the risk mechanism? • Can mediators be extrapolated to other populations and contexts?
Program Theory	• Cross-cultural relevance of problem structure and program theory • Evidence from efficacy and effectiveness trials	• Does evidence suggest that the program is applicable across cultures, settings, sites, and populations for which no data are available? • Is there evidence that program theory – risk factors, protective factors, and mediators – is different across cultures, settings, sites, and populations? • Does the intervention have high potential for uptake on measures of diffusion such as relative advantage, comparability, complexity, trialability, and observability (see Chapter 6)?

Training	• Program and training materials extrapolated for diffusion
	• Cultural and contextual congruence of program materials
	• Materials for training or certification of intervention agents
	  – Screening and recruitment materials
	  – Training materials
		• Are program materials widely available at a reasonable cost?
		• Do program materials provide instructions for cultural and contextual adaptation where it may be advisable?
		• Are standards regarding implementation clear? Are standards measurable? Are implementation measures available?
		• Is training readily available and adequate?
		• Is a user-certification process needed?

Continued

Table 4.4 Stage 4: Translation and Adaptation of Program Manuals and Related Materials (*Continued*)

Section	Content Areas	Considerations
	– Internship or supervised practicum guidelines – Proficiency examinations – Available reimbursement mechanisms, supportive public policies, and other contextual conditions affecting diffusion	• Do reimbursement schema provide a mechanism to pay for the program?
Format	• Professional development and training, including certification • Web-based access to program materials, video, and training	• How should training or certificate programs be organized in order to extend reach and promote diffusion?
Adapting Session Content	• Clear specification of essential activities or intervention content • Procedures and guidelines for translation and adaptation • Suggestions for ways content may be adapted for cultural congruence	• Is essential, distinguishing content identified? • Is there a recommended process for translating and adapting content (e.g., translation is independently reviewed; activities are adapted by a panel of culture and program experts)? • Are examples included of content adapted for different cultures, settings, venues, sites, or populations?

no data were available on the relevance of its core construct (skills in social information processing) to children in China. However, data were available suggesting that social information processing is similar among children from different cultures in the United States and Europe. Those data gave us initial confidence that program theory might have broad cultural application and that the *Making Choices* program might work in China. At the same time, experts in child development and government officials responsible for program development in China were invited to observe *Making Choices* in U.S. schools. A group of Chinese educators, administrators, and scholars visited the United States and watched teachers use *Making Choices* in their classrooms. After three such observations by different groups, the Chinese government decided to fund a translation and adaptation task force comprised of Chinese and American experts.

Seven social work and social science faculty members from Nankai University in Tianjin, worked on the *Making Choices* translation and adaptation project. Collectively, they reviewed the Chinese research literature, much of which had not penetrated Western journals, to assess the cross-cultural validity of program theory. Their job was both to translate *Making Choices* and to identify ways to strengthen the cultural relevance of the lessons for children in China. Relying on culturally relevant studies and their observations of *Making Choices*, they identified adaptations that would enhance the relevance of program activities.

Translation, Back-Translation, and Consensual Re-Translation

After program theory is found relevant and ideas for adaptation begin to emerge, program materials must be translated formally to the language of implementation—that is, the language to be used by practitioners in providing the intervention. The goal of translation is to create program materials that are semantically equivalent to the original program materials. Therefore, as opposed to literal translation, conceptual equivalence translation seeks comparable, culturally anchored meaning.

At this level, translation is an iterative process that often involves a team of linguists *and* program experts. Translation must be done with care because program materials are often nuanced by idiomatic expressions. Indeed, there may be ten ways to translate a word or a phrase (e.g., "Terrell told Lucius, 'This game will knock your socks off.'"), but there may be only one way that conveys the meaning intended by the program developers. In the end, translation should communicate culturally nuanced meanings of all core constructs, and program content should be rooted in activities that are culturally familiar. This requires an iterative sequential process involving initial independent translation by at least two linguists, and back-translation into English (back-translation is the process of translating a document that has already been translated into a foreign language back into the original language, preferably using different translators for each version). For example, if English was the language in which program materials were initially developed, different linguists working on the translation and back-translation are more likely to identify problematic wording (e.g., mistranslation of idiomatic expressions such as "knock your socks off"). When problems are identified, the linguists then discuss the issue to reach consensus on the proper translation (Brislin 1970; Guillemin, Bombardier, and Beaton 1993; van Widenfelt, Treffers, de Beurs, Siebelink, and Koudijs 2005). The goal of this collective translation process is to identify words and phrases that best capture both the meaning and cultural shading of phrases and words used in the original program materials.

Cultural Adaptation of Core Constructs and Program Activities

After a translation is agreed on, the process of cultural adaptation may begin. Cultural adaptation is the organized and rational process of tailoring a program to the idioms of everyday life in a target population. To be meaningful, content must have colloquial relevance. A program must have currency and clarity—it must not feel alien. Concepts must be in keeping with prevailing values and beliefs and with the missions of the organizations (e.g., agencies, schools, health clinics, and neighborhood centers) in which programs are to be delivered. Activities should not prompt resistance. Indeed, activities should engender motivation and be syncopated to the rhythms of the setting.

Two forms of adaptation should be considered: program delivery and program content (Castro, Barrera, and Martinez 2004). The logical first step is to determine the form of program delivery. In adapting the

Making Choices program for China, one of our first concerns was, given the vastly different approaches to teaching used in U.S. and Chinese schools, whether Chinese schools could support this form of prevention programming. Our concern was primarily based on the fact that *Making Choices* uses a highly interactive approach that is unfamiliar to many teachers in Chinese schools. Working with Chinese colleagues, we visited schools, explained the *Making Choices* program, and solicited the opinions of principals and teachers on the form of program delivery. This included discussion of the roles of teachers and principals, the views and roles of parents, and the importance of political representatives within Chinese schools and neighborhoods. The process also involved developing an understanding of neighborhood cooperatives and other community organizations that might have a stake in providing the *Making Choices* program. Initially, cultural adaptation involves a full environmental scan.

The goal of adaptation is to select a means for program delivery that will maximize the reach to the target population and provide assurance of implementation with fidelity. Initially, the focus of the adaptation process is on identifying the available mechanisms for providing a program. The auspices and responsibilities of social institutions such as schools often vary across cultures. For example, in China schools have little history of providing social and character education. Over the past 50 years, social education was done principally through neighborhood cooperatives and an extensive system of political officers who provided both formal social control and social support at the community level. Moreover, education in China relies more on directed learning and memorization and less on interactive learning. In addition to the concern based on the *Making Choices* interactive learning format, the program is designed to be used by a school social worker, school psychologist, school counselor, or teacher. However, China has no school social workers, psychologists, or counselors. Given these fundamental differences, the adaptation team was unsure whether *Making Choices* could be delivered in public schools, and team members made many visits to schools to evaluate the potential setting. In addition, adaptation team members visited another potential program setting—the neighborhood centers (formerly cooperatives), where paraprofessionals staff after-school programs, run health clinics, provide in-home services, and organize a variety of recreational activities. In the end, the team decided that most Chinese teachers were interested in learning interactional teaching methods and that the *Making Choices* program could be supplemented with teacher training materials on peer social dynamics, small group learning, and classroom behavior management. After translation, cultural adaptation includes understanding the service provision system, organizational structures, staffing patterns, and capabilities of potential intervention agents.

The second activity defining a systematic approach to cultural adaptation involves selection and modification of program content to improve fit—but without compromising the core features of program theory. This activity also requires a collaborative sequential process involving culture and program experts. Together, the experts identify content that is culturally relevant and distinguish it from content that should be modified. This process can produce interesting discussions. For example, one exercise in *Making Choices* involves a baseball story. Baseball is not a familiar sport in China. However, Nankai faculty members on the adaptation team were split in their views on whether a more familiar sport, such as basketball, should be substituted for baseball. Some argued that it would be good for Chinese children to learn about baseball. Others argued that learning about baseball, while valuable, was not the intent of *Making Choices* and that basketball (or soccer) should be used because the substitution would permit practitioners to focus on explaining core social information processing concepts rather than an American sport. The latter view eventually prevailed. This process of identifying program content that may have poor fit, discussing it from the perspective of culture, and developing alternative content requires knowledge of the way program mechanisms (i.e., mediators) may or may not operate within a target population.

Conclusion

This chapter focused on Step 2 in intervention research: Create and Revise Program Materials. Although much of the work in designing and developing program materials occurs in Step 2, it does not exclusively take place in this step. Indeed, it is spread out across each of the five steps of intervention research. To represent this work as a cross-cutting activity in intervention research, we described four stages in the development of intervention manuals and other program materials: formulation of materials, revision of materials, differentiation in the intended setting, and translation/adaptation for new settings. Formulation builds on activities to develop problem and program theories in Step 1 of intervention research. Revision and differentiation draw on pilot tests, expert reviews, and controlled trials conducted in Step 3 and Step 4 of intervention research. Central to dissemination in Step 5, translation and cultural adaptation require reassessment of delivery mechanisms and program content.

Once developed, a program manual contains sequenced content that spells out goals, objectives, and activities. A manual defines a systematic change strategy. Outlined in the text box below, manuals should describe the problem(s) for which the intervention was created, and specify both proximal goals—such as changes in skills, and distal goals—such as changes in social or health problems. A target population is identified. The system level of intervention is stated; that is, whether the intervention targets the problem at the level of the individual, family, group, organization, community, or a combination of levels. Manuals should articulate program theories (comprised of logic models or theories of change), key points of intervention, mediating factors or mechanisms, and desired results. The format of delivery of the intervention should be discussed. This may include the manner in which the intervention is presented, such as lecture, discussion, homework, or other forms of action; the interaction format, such as face-to-face, telephone, or Internet; or the type of leadership, such as leader, co-leaders of the same profession or of different professions, and member-leader. The duration and frequency of sessions are specified.

In addition, the practice skills necessary to carry out the intervention should also be described. Skills such as establishing a therapeutic alliance, guiding group process, and engaging different facets of a community may be crucial in implementing the activities of a new intervention.

Key Components of an Intervention Manual

Introduction

- Describe the problem being addressed
- Review incidence or prevalence data (i.e., discuss who experiences the problem)
- Discuss the need or rationale for an intervention
- Specify a logic model and/or a theory of change, including a description of the mediating mechanisms that are malleable
- Describe the intervention format and recommend strategies for using program materials
- Optional: Provide or refer to a literature review on which program theory is based

Intervention Sessions

Must determine

- System level of change (community, organization, family, group, individual)
- System level of implementation (community, organization, family, group, individual)
- Duration and frequency of intervention sessions
- Setting (where intervention is delivered)
- Method of delivery (lecture, hands on activities, video)
- Intervention agent (who delivers the intervention)
- Mode of intervention (face-to-face, telephone, computer)

The manual must provide

- Goals, objectives, and content for each session
- Suggestions for adapting content on the basis of race/ethnicity, culture, language, religion, or other factors
- Decision rules for choices among alternative interventions, if applicable

(continued)

- Directions for inclusion of essential versus enrichment or supplemental content
- Details of specific intervention activities
- Guidelines for selection of participants
- Description of proximal outcomes and distal outcomes
- Standards for training and supervision of practitioners

Resources for Facilitators

- Screening and recruitment materials
- Examples of scripted dialogue

The manual itself may contain specific information about ways to manage group process, to deal with common problems in implementation, or to anticipate the effects of the intervention on an organization.

Thus, treatment manuals present content and a sequence of activities that comprise an intervention. Although we have outlined what we consider to be distinct stages of manual development and the features that should be included in fully designed manuals, manuals currently used in practice are often less complete in design than in the suggested template. We have described a design and development process that can only be completed with significant financial support. It represents an ideal.

Finally, we concentrated on manuals that are designed as part of intervention research. To be sure, manuals also may be developed outside a research enterprise. When intervention research cannot be carried out, practitioners and students may want to work on a manual that will lead to intervention research. We encourage this—to codify and standardize current interventions. In the long run, manuals must be tested. In the next chapter, we describe this testing process by reviewing both efficacy and effectiveness trials, which constitute Step 3 and Step 4 in the intervention research process.

Appendix 4.1

What Is a Goal?
(Problem Solving Step #3: Setting Goals)

Objectives:

The learner will be able to identify three goals when presented with a description of a simple social situation.

The learner will use oral and written language to present information in a sequenced, logical manner and to share information and ideas.

Materials:

Solve Problems the Making Choices Way poster
Situation Cards, Is It a Goal? worksheet

Introduction:

Review the *Solve Problems the Making Choices Way* poster and tell students they have now conquered the first two steps in the sequence. They have learned how to find clues and how to decide what the clues mean. They will now move on to the third step, *Forming a Goal*. Explain that in the next few lessons they will be learning how to determine what they want to happen and how to set a goal. Ask the students to define the word *goal*; then read the following definition and write it on the board: *A goal is something a person wants.*

Read the following examples of goals to the class:

Annie wants a new soccer ball.

Luis wants to buy a new basketball hoop.

Sadie wants to have fun at a party.

James wants to get an "A" on the math test.

Anthony wants to make friends with a new person in his class.

Individual

Activity I:

Point out that we set goals all the time by deciding what we want to accomplish. Sometimes a goal involves getting something we do not currently have, at other times goals involve wanting to keep something that we already have—this can be an object (e.g., a cool CD), a friend, or a feeling. Ask students for some examples of goals they have set for themselves. Call on students to share their examples.

Pass out the sheet *Is It a Goal?* Explain to students that they will place an X beside the sentences that are goals.

Whole Class

Activity II: Identifying the Problem and Setting a Goal

Create the following chart on chart paper or on a transparency:

SITUATION/ PROBLEM	GOALS
My brother took my favorite CD and won't give it back.	To get my CD back without fighting with him. Or Let him keep it and see if I can get something from him in return.

Read aloud one of the *Situation Cards*. After reading the card, ask the students to identify the situation or problem. Then have students decide on several different goals that will help solve the problem. Focus on generating multiple goals for each situation. Repeat the process for each of the *Situation Cards.*

Conclusion:

Review the idea that a goal is something we want to happen, to obtain, or something we have that we want to keep. In order to reach our goal, we must decide what action steps must be accomplished.

Activity Sheet I

Is It a Goal?

A GOAL is something we want to do or get.
We set goals BEFORE we act.
Read each sentence below carefully. Decide if the sentence is a GOAL or not. Place an X next to the sentences that are GOALS.

1. _____ Julie wants to earn an "A" on her spelling test.
2. _____ Miguel asked his teacher for help.
3. _____ Phil would like to earn extra money to buy his favorite video game.
4. _____ Amy wants to make more friends at school.
5. _____ Melissa invited her friend over for dinner.
6. _____ Mario wants to try out for the baseball team.
7. _____ Antonia rode the bus home from school.
8. _____ Martin would like to learn to dive off the high dive at the pool.

9. _____ Maria helped her mother pick out a gift for her grandmother.

10. _____ Trey wants to go to the movies.

Activity II

Situation Cards

The student next to you copies off your paper.	You hear Anna telling another girl that she is not going to invite you to her birthday party.	Your best friend tells you she cheated on the social studies test yesterday.
During a basketball game in gym, you accidentally hit the meanest kid in class in the nose.	Without asking, Jamie goes into your desk and takes your favorite pencil.	Tom tells everyone at school that when he was visiting at John's house, he heard John's parents fighting.
You see Jennifer asking all the girls in your class to play a special game at recess, but she doesn't ask you.	You have tickets to see a great movie, but you don't know which of your two best friends to invite to come with you.	You want to go hang out with your friend. You need your father's permission to go to your friend's house, but you just had an argument with your father.
Your buddy has to go home early, but you have permission to stay at the playground for another hour. You see a bunch of kids you don't know playing ball.	A new kid at school reaches for the last piece of cake in the cafeteria just as you were reaching for it.	Two friends you haven't seen in a while ask you if you want to check out the CDs they just swiped.

5

Step 3 and Step 4: From Refining Program Components to Testing Effectiveness

This chapter describes Steps 3 and 4 of the five-step intervention research process. Step 3 involves refining and confirming program components through efficacy testing. Step 4 focuses on effectiveness testing in which the effects of interventions are assessed in a variety of settings and circumstances. More broadly, this chapter tells the story of why we evaluate social interventions using the logic of experimentation; how to begin with small, inexpensive pilot tests to help refine program components; and how to expand the effort to conduct an efficacy test with high-quality implementation. We conclude by discussing the challenges of relaxing control over programs and testing effectiveness under routine practice conditions.

One of the basic maxims of practice is the need to allocate scarce resources to their best use. That is the rationale for trying to understand the value of social and health interventions before committing resources to one program over another. In a curious way, we found this competition for resources in our work as we developed the *Making Choices* program for elementary schools. School principals and teachers whom we approached were interested in new methods to prevent aggressive behavior, especially teasing and bullying. In most cases, the classroom management techniques they used were not working well and some children repeatedly disrupted class despite behavior contracts, consistent consequences, and trips to the assistant principal's office. At the same time, principals and teachers (and our research team) also viewed class time as a scarce resource with many competing uses. As stakeholders in the education of the students, teachers wanted to know what types of outcomes they could expect from the *Making Choices* program—Were they likely to see reductions in social aggression and classroom disruptions? Should they expect to see improved class communication and dynamics? Moreover, the teachers also had questions about how much effort they would have to invest in the program: how much time out of the thirty-hour school week "budget" would a teacher spend on in-service training, how much time lecturing on new concepts, how much time for in-class activities and homework, how much out-of-class preparation time would *Making Choices* require each week? To address these concerns, the intervention team undertook a series of studies intended to refine program components and improve fit with the practice setting (in this case, the classroom).

A Sequence of Tests

Developing a full understanding of the impact of an intervention requires a sequence of studies. Let's look at the example of what is involved in the development of a new drug therapy. Before a drug is approved for general distribution, it is tested to make sure that it provides a benefit and does not have any harmful effects (or at least falls within an acceptable level of possible side effects). Medical researchers construct experiments with optimum conditions to show that use of the drug causes specific positive outcomes. In these studies, the medical researchers carefully control every aspect of the testing, including controlling the quality of the drug; setting the screening criteria for patients allowed into the study (rejecting potential participants whose data might confound the results, such as those with co-occurring conditions); determining the dosage and frequency with which the drug is administered (directly managing the delivery of the drug to prevent missed doses); and monitoring of all other health-related activity during the trial. To assess the drug's impact, medical researchers use an evaluation design that will support the causal inference that the use of the new drug best explains the observed differences at the end of the trial. Standard procedure in medical research calls for use of randomized controlled trials (RCTs) in which study participants are randomly assigned to either the treatment or the control group. In addition, protocols for drug trials allow researchers to use procedures that keep participants unaware of their group assignment (e.g., by giving a placebo drug to the control group), which prevents a participant's knowledge of group assignment from affecting his or her behavior in a way that would influence outcomes. If a drug passes this trial, it commences to the next phase of testing in regular clinical settings. This next test is to determine whether the results hold up when doctors are given control over prescribing the drug and patients are allowed to monitor their own compliance (or noncompliance) with dosage instructions and complementary health behavior guides (Do they skip doses? Do they take the medicine as long as they are supposed to? Do they follow directions to curtail activities that interfere with the drug?). The results of this effectiveness trial will tell the researcher if the indications for the drug are correct, if unsupervised doctors prescribe the drug properly, and if the directions to the patient are clear and reasonable. In short, an effectiveness trial indicates how much effect can be expected when the drug is used under routine practice conditions rather than ideal conditions.

We use the same basic sequence of tests in social and behavioral research. However, unlike many drug trials examining the effects of a single agent, social and behavioral interventions are complicated. Sociobehavioral investigations often involve combinations of approaches, and consist of procedures that are not easily standardized. When an intervention is a collection of practices and procedures (rather than a single pill), it is challenging to assign observed effects to the proper component. In addition, in many practice settings it is not possible or ethical to assign participants to a no-treatment control. Therefore, the *treatment-as-usual*

(TAU) condition (i.e., routine services) is now accepted as the standard control or comparison condition in social and behavior research. Thus, socio- and behavior-oriented intervention research tends to measure the relative advantage of an intervention as compared to routine services, rather than the difference between treatment and no-treatment (and researchers must specify and measure the content of both the treatment and the TAU protocols; for more on this see the Fidelity section below). Finally, the mechanisms that drive social problems are often less well understood than the biological processes of illness; therefore, the formulation of a program theory that specifies mediators and focuses intervention involves greater speculation. Often, we must specify several plausible mediating processes, and this leads to complex, multielement interventions. As social researchers, we face challenges that are in many ways quite different from those faced by biomedical researchers.

So to test these complex social programs, researchers have established standards of evidence for measuring program processes and outcomes. This chapter describes how evaluation questions and designs change as the research progresses from Step 3 (refining and confirming program components) to Step 4 (effectiveness testing in a variety of practice settings). First, we examine the logic of experimentation, causal inference, and standards of validity. Next, building on Chapter 4, we expand the discussion of pilot testing and address types of study designs, the value of mixed methods in pilot tests, and we provide a case study to illustrate how pilot testing allows the researcher to monitor the training, supervision, and coaching of the intervention agents. Finally, we build on the discussion of the sequencing of testing and examine *efficacy testing* and *effectiveness testing* as related to issues of implementation and adaptation.

The Logic of Experimentation

Ultimately, intervention research is intended to show that programs produce desirable social or health outcomes. We want to make the inference that an intervention produced a particular outcome. In short, we want to make a causal argument.

Causal inference must meet the following basic requirements: the cause must precede the effect, the cause must vary (covary or be correlated) with the effect, and alternative explanations for the effect must be implausible (Shadish, Cook, and Campbell 2002). The classic example is a chemist dipping an iron bar into a jar of acid. When the bar dissolves, the cause (dipping in acid) can be seen to precede the effect (dissolving). The cause can be observed to covary with the effect (the iron does not dissolve when it is not dipped and stops dissolving when removed from the acid). In addition, we know enough from our experience with iron objects to rule out alternative explanations (iron does not dissolve on its own). Findings from an experiment that meets these three criteria of causal inference are described as having *internal validity*.

In Chapter 3 we described how social researchers use problem theory and logic models to separate outcomes of interest into categories of *distal* outcomes such as school dropout, arrest, or child maltreatment, and the intermediate effect of *proximal* (i.e., shorter term) outcomes such as school attachment, aggressive behavior, and parenting skill. Researchers also seek evidence of mediating processes that can be invisible to direct observation (e.g., changing knowledge, beliefs, motivation or readiness to change, or cognitive skills) to learn more about the mechanisms that produce an intervention's desired changes. Experiments in social research strive to achieve internal validity within the framework of causal inference. When designing an experimental test, social researchers set up a situation where the cause in question (the program) precedes the observed effects. Then they use statistical analysis to show the covariance of cause and effect, including the covariation of mediators with outcomes. The research design (i.e., the specifics of the experimental procedures) is itself the mechanism that makes it possible to reject plausible alternative explanations of the observed effects.

Research Design

Research design is the process of specifying who will receive an intervention and how outcomes will be observed. As discussed in Chapter 2, a design defines the core elements of research studies such as which participants will make up treatment and control groups (or conditions), and what measures will be used for the dependent and other variables. In addition, research design indicates when an intervention occurs and specifies over what period it will be provided. Figure 5.1 illustrates the common experimental pre-test–post-test design using standard notation. The figure should be read left to right to show the passage of time. The two rows represent two groups of participants, and the R indicates that participants are randomly assigned to conditions. Each O represents an assessment point when a measure (e.g., a survey, a questionnaire, a test) is given to the participants. The stacked Os represents two waves (two rounds) of measures given to the two groups at the same point in time. The X stands for the introduction of the intervention between the two sets of observations.

Figure 5.1 is only one example of an array of different designs developed to address a variety of research questions. The goal is always to select a design that will result in valid inferences given the circumstances. Because the procedures specified in the design form a mechanism for rejecting plausible alternative explanations, different designs are used to address rival hypotheses. In addition, different designs are needed to deal with ethical constraints (e.g., when withholding treatment from the comparison group is not ethical), resource limitations (e.g., when a large sample is not feasible), and time limits (e.g., when repeated pretests or follow-up observations are precluded). Moreover, because research always involves compromises, the selection of a design often represents a decision to emphasize internal validity at the expense of external validity. In other words, sometimes the researcher has to choose between placing emphasis on causal inference (internal validity) over the desire to generalize

$$
\begin{array}{cccc}
R & O & X & O \\
\hline
R & O &   & O \\
\end{array}
$$

Figure 5.1 Research design notation.

the results to various contexts (external validity). The selection of an evaluation design always involves tradeoffs (Shadish *et al.* 2002, 35).

Experimental Designs in Intervention Research

In intervention research, we often think of two basic types of research designs: experimental and quasi-experimental designs. Experimental designs are distinguished by the use of random assignment to create intervention and control groups. With large enough groups random assignment usually produces between-group equivalence on both observed and unobserved measures. No other method of group assignment and no method of statistical adjustment produces similar effects. When randomization is used, between-group post-intervention differences can be considered causally related to the intervention—assuming no post randomization effects are confounded with the treatment effect.

Criteria for the *goodness* of research designs have been established by the National Institutes of Health, the Society for Prevention Research (SPR), and other professional organizations. For example, to meet the standard for causal inference under the SPR criteria (2004), studies must have both (1) a comparison condition receiving no treatment, usual care, placebo, or wait list; and (2) an assignment mechanism that maximizes confidence that the intervention causes the reported outcomes and that selection biases are minimized.

The term *selection bias* refers to nonrandom assignment processes that result in group differences not caused by the intervention. When selection bias occurs, inferences about the effect of an intervention are biased because the groups are not balanced on key characteristics. That is, measured effects at the end of the study may not be caused solely or even partly by the program but merely represent preintervention differences between the treatment and the control groups. In other words, selection bias affects the validity of inferences about the effect of interventions. The between-group differences that produce selection bias include significant sociodemographic variation or other characteristics such as cumulative risk, or motivation to participate in the research. Consider the example of a study comparing routine cancer treatment in a hospital setting to naturopathic cancer treatment that is implemented in a health center specializing in alternative medical treatments. Such a study will encounter significant selection bias because the patient population coming to the specialized center will be biased toward those seeking alternative treatments and will not be representative of the larger population. Controlling selection biases usually requires random assignment, although other designs are acceptable under specific conditions (e.g., interrupted time series and regression discontinuity designs, which are discussed later in this chapter), including when it may not be ethical to assign participants to one versus another treatment. As mentioned above, *post-randomization effects* represent another factor that can compromise between-group equivalence. These effects range from events that differentially affect one group (e.g., attrition from the control group but not the intervention group) to reactions to randomization (e.g., John Henry effects, a situation in which control group participants become aware of their assignment to the control condition and compete to out-achieve participants in intervention conditions). Though post-randomization effects are not technically related to the selection mechanism, they are sometimes considered sources of selection bias because they affect group equivalence. (For more information on pre- and post-randomization threats to validity, see Shadish *et al.* [2002].)

Quasi-Experimental Designs in Intervention Research

Quasi-experimental designs have the same aims and most of the same structural features as true experimental designs. Both have intervention groups and both measure dependent variables in relation to the treatment. However, the key difference is in the assignment of participants to groups. In place of the random assignment found in experimental designs, in quasi-experimental design groups—if there are two groups—are assigned by nonrandom means including self-selection (e.g., when participants who volunteer to participate in an intervention are compared to participants who do not volunteer for an intervention) or selection by administrative means (e.g., when the researcher assigns the first 50 enrollees to the treatment group and the next 50 to the comparison group).

By using nonrandom assignment, quasi-experimental designs are exposed to a variety of potential biases including selection bias, also called *selection effects*. These may occur because self-selected or administratively selected groups have characteristics that create plausible rival explanations for observed differences between intervention participants and those in a comparison group. For example, participants self-selected to receive an intervention may be more willing to change a behavior. In a study involving smokers, self-selected participants in an intervention are likely to be more interested in changing their behavior than participants who do not volunteer for the intervention.

Consider a *cohort study* that compares third-grade students in two successive years. Students in the first-year cohort receive no intervention, whereas students in the second-year cohort receive an intervention. This investigation uses a quasi-experimental design because the students are not randomly assigned into cohorts (year 1 versus year 2), nor are they randomly assigned to classrooms. Systematic differences between the two cohorts could lurk in unexpected places. For example, a beloved principal may leave the school. History events have the potential to provide a plausible alternative explanation for an observed difference between students in Cohort 1 (i.e., the end of year 1) and students in Cohort 2 (i.e., students in the same classrooms the following year).

When using a quasi-experimental design, the researcher's job is to identify and rule out potential alternative explanations. Using measurements taken over time, some quasi-experimental designs do this well. For example, when the researcher establishes a baseline through a series of measurements, it is often possible to chart the effect of a new program or policy as an interruption in the baseline. This is called an *interrupted time-series design*. In addition, it may be possible to measure participants on a key indicator, such as cumulative risk, and then to provide an intervention only to those participants who reach a certain threshold level on the measure. The difference in the regression lines (intercepts and slopes) between the two groups can provide evidence for a program effect. This approach is called a *regression discontinuity design*. Findings from both interrupted times-series and regression discontinuity designs can have high validity (Doss and Atkins 2006). Unfortunately, these designs are rarely used in social work. Instead, designs without comparison conditions tend to dominate social work research. Findings from these designs are tortuously difficult to interpret (and do not meet high-quality design criteria such as those of the Society for Prevention Research).

Using experimental and quasi-experimental methods, intervention research is distinguished by a sequence that begins with pilot tests and concludes with effectiveness tests or trials. In the context of causal inference, this sequence of tests can be thought of as a systematic attempt to demonstrate the utility of an intervention and refine its approach with the goal of building an understanding of the intervention's impact on mediators, proximal outcomes, and distal events. In the case study below, notice how the researcher's role changes over time.

Case Study: Preventing Infection in ICUs

Hospital intensive care units (ICUs) treat victims of devastating events—drowning, gunshots, burns, falls, aneurisms, and cardiac arrest. ICUs apply specialized technologies and therapies to take over critical body functions that have failed—ventilators to replace lungs, dialysis to replace kidneys, and even aortic pumps to replace failed hearts. Use of intensive care has risen steeply as the range of treatable conditions grows, which in turn is a function of new technology.

As medicine harnesses more technology to treat serious injuries and illnesses, the complexity of ICU medicine grows as well. Thousands of procedures, mechanisms, and medications have to be organized and sequenced to treat hundreds of conditions. Failure to manage the complexity is normal (Gawande 2007), and this failure results in infections, setbacks, complications, and death.

At the Johns Hopkins Hospital in Baltimore, Dr. Peter Pronovost recognized the problem of managing this complexity for hundreds of interlocking ICU procedures and decided to try out a simple new remedy. He came up with a checklist of the proper steps for just one common procedure: putting an intravenous catheter line into a patient. Annual ICU bloodstream infections from catheters have been estimated at

80,000, resulting in 28,000 deaths and \$2.3 billion in added treatment costs (Pronovost *et al.* 2006). The checklist had five steps: (1) wash your hands; (2) clean the patient's skin with a specified antiseptic; (3) drape the rest of the patient's body; (4) wear sterile gloves, mask, and gown; and (5) cover the catheter with a sterile dressing.

Dr. Pronovost's idea to solve a health problem was based on a clear specification of the source of most infections. That is, the mediator was defined as exposure to infection during the catheterization process. However, as an intervention, the checklist still required testing to prove that it worked. After all, ICU doctors and nurses might have better ways to allocate their scarce time than filling out somewhat obvious checklists. One doctor's reaction was, "Forget the paperwork. Take care of the patient!" (Gawande 2007).

The first thing Pronovost did was to give his checklist to the ICU nurses and ask them to observe doctors for a month. The nurses were to keep data on the doctors' catheter procedures by marking how often all five steps were completed. More than a third of the time, the doctors skipped at least one step.

Next, Pronovost presented the results of these observations to the ICU team, instituted the checklist as a required procedure, and empowered the nurses to remind the doctors of the steps to ensure all steps were completed. Over the next year, the infection rate went from 11% to 0. Pronovost's team extended the trial another fifteen months—in which there were only two infections compared to the forty-five that were expected based on past infection rates. Pronovost's team estimated that eight deaths had been prevented and \$2 million saved in the ICU.

But would this approach work in a hospital where Dr. Pronovost was not present to reinforce the use of the checklist, to convince doctors that the extra paperwork had value, and to support nurses who intervened when doctors skipped steps? To answer this question, the Michigan Health and Hospital Association signed up to try the checklist in ICUs across the state. At first, the ICUs established a baseline by tracking only their own infection rates, which showed they were above the national average. Then, each hospital assigned a project manager who provided the checklists to staff and talked to the Johns Hopkins team once a month.

In addition, each hospital named a senior executive to visit the ICU, monitor the project, solve problems, and get feedback.

The results were both immediate and dramatic. In the first three months of the checklist project, the infection rate fell 66%. In the first 18 months, the project saved an estimated $275 million and 1,500 lives. Now other states and the nation of Spain are implementing the checklist. Dr. Pronovost has begun testing checklists for other procedures.

Step 3: Refining and Confirming Program Components

Intervention research is an iterative and sequential process that begins with an idea that informs the design of a program, progresses though pilot testing to tests of impact, and concludes with dissemination. Here we discuss the pilot testing phase that refines program components, differentiates content based on context and culture, and estimates program impacts in a variety of settings.

Pilot Testing an Intervention after Initial Development

Step 3 begins with pilot testing in small, often single-group or single-case studies with measures of both intervention processes and proximal outcomes. The goals of pilot testing are to (1) develop and refine an intervention in the context of practice, and (2) to collect preliminary evidence of change in mediators and proximal outcomes. Achieving these goals often involves a community participatory process, meaning that a variety of stakeholders are involved in developing the research questions, delivering the intervention, collecting data, and interpreting outcomes. For example, in the case of the ICU checklist, Dr. Pronovost involved nurses, fellow doctors, and administrators. The design in pilot testing is relatively simple, and nearly always quasi-experimental. Pilot tests generally involve a single group of participants who are aware that they are part of a pilot test. Indeed, researchers may even ask the study participants to give feedback on program activities or the procedures used in the intervention.

Shown in Table 5.1, pilot testing requires both qualitative and quantitative measurements. Data collection and analyses focus on understanding the responses of participants to program content, including whether activities engage participants and seem to produce change in mediators. In the initial testing of *Making Choices* we ran a single-group test and interviewed the intervention agent (a psychologist who served as

Table 5.1 Stages of Testing: Pilot, Efficacy, and Effectiveness Studies

Pilot studies	Efficacy studies	Effectiveness studies
Participants		
Small convenience sample	Homogenous, often motivated sample; exclude those with complications, other comorbid problems	Broad, heterogeneous sample, often use a defined population
Intervention type		
Novel intervention or new adaptation of existing program, modified and refined even during the study	Problem-focused interventions that attempt to maximize effect size, high fidelity	Tested interventions; often manualized
Evaluation design		
Single group or case control design	Randomized designs	Randomized or quasi-experimental design
Organizational context		
One setting allowing high access to staff for process evaluation	Usually one setting to reduce variability; settings with many resources and expert staff	Appeal to and work in multiple settings; able to be adapted to fit setting
Implementation		
Implemented by research staff with close monitoring and qualitative feedback; protocol refinement in progress	Implemented by research staff closely following specific protocol	Implemented by variety of different staff following specific protocol

Source: Adapted from Glasgow, Lichtenstein, and Marcus, 2003. Used with permission.

group leader), group members, teachers, and parents. In a subsequent study, we conducted focus groups with teachers, who served as intervention agents, and asked them to review program content that they judged as either "effective" or "not very effective." We then used the information to revise program activities and to develop new content. Because sample sizes in pilot testing are usually small, quantitative measurement may not be as useful as mixed methods approaches. When quantitative measures are used, frequent data collection on a few measures may be preferable to pre- and posttesting on a broad array of measures. Measurement should begin with repeated pretests well before introducing the intervention and continue during intervention; this amount of data allows for plotting of key variables before, during, and after exposure to program content. Small pilot tests make intensive measurement a feasible approach.

Efficacy Test: Refining and Confirming Program Components

After a program has been designed and pilot tested, we want to know whether it works. That is, based on program theory, does the program produce change in the mediators and do the changes in mediators appear to produce changes in proximal outcomes? Efficacy tests strive to maximize causal inference by using designs that eliminate common alternative explanations for program effects. These designs involve random assignment of participants to program conditions and control groups, or they may use strong quasi-experimental methods such as regression discontinuity designs.

An efficacy test requires a program model to be well specified. Following the manual development process described in Chapter 4, at the point of initiating efficacy tests the program manual and materials must be complete and ready to use in practice, because the treatment must be stable and replicable. However, having fully developed materials does not preclude further revision based on the efficacy tests as well as later trials of the program. High quality provision of the program is also important for an efficacy test. Interruptions in the availability of the program during the test, or poor implementation, will confound results.

Finally, inclusion and exclusion criteria are often used to screen program participants to ensure that they represent the target population.

Step 4: Assessing Effectiveness in a Variety of Settings and Circumstances

Efficacy testing is followed by effectiveness testing, whose purpose is to estimate the impact of the intervention under real-world practice conditions. That is, effectiveness trials are designed to see whether the impact of an intervention can generalize to practice when the wraparound support (e.g., high administrative and organizational support, extensive training and supervision of intervention agents) of an efficacy trial are no longer available. A program that has been shown to achieve the desired impact under the ideal conditions of an efficacy trial is now exposed to other settings that represent the diversity of practice conditions for which the program was intended. Effectiveness trials test the implementation model of the program, including the program materials and manuals, training modules, and other means of specifying an intervention. Unlike efficacy tests, two conditions are relaxed in effectiveness tests: provision of the program is no longer under the direct control of the researcher, and the adherence of participants to the treatment is subject to natural variation.

Intent to Treat Analyses

Effectiveness trials use forms of analysis (e.g., intent to treat and dose response) that take into account the program implementation. Intent to treat (ITT) is an approach that counts the results of all participants assigned to the treatment group equally, whether they received a full or partial dose of the program. ITT includes the results of people who dropped out alongside the often-better results of motivated participants who completed the intervention. ITT analyses ask the question: What was the impact of the program on the intended population? These kinds of analyses recognize that programs will inevitably lose some of the people that the program was intended to treat. People will drop out, attend sporadically, or attend but fail to comply with treatment. Assuming that this kind of variation would occur in real-world practice, ITT analyses yield effect estimates for the target population and not merely for those who complete an intervention. ITT produces estimates of expected effects that will be relevant to policy makers who are concerned with the effect of a program when it is brought to scale.

Efficacy Subset or Treatment of the Treated Analyses

Dose response analyses estimate treatment outcomes based on the amount of treatment received. In these analyses, outcomes for participants who receive the full intervention are compared with outcomes for participants in a control or comparison group. This comparison involves selecting a subset of participants in the intervention condition; hence, it is often called *efficacy subset analysis*. When this comparison involves estimating a treatment effect for participants who (by some criterion) are considered to be fully treated, it is also called *treatment of the treated*. Efficacy subset results carry the caution of likely self-selection bias because it is usually the case that greater exposure is correlated with greater motivation. Thus, the fully treated group is likely to differ from the comparison group in a way that could influence outcomes. New statistical methods (such as *propensity score matching or weighting*) are being developed to address this problem and they hold the potential to create equivalence between efficacy subsets and matched participants in the control or comparison groups. These new methods are described briefly in Chapter 7, and we recommend Guo and Fraser (in press) for a full discussion.

We now turn our attention to measurement issues that confront researchers during pilot tests, efficacy trials, and effectiveness studies. We describe a mixed methods approach and advocate for the use of both quantitative and qualitative measurement. Three cross-cutting topics are addressed: the measurement of outcomes, program implementation, and program fidelity. We conclude the chapter with a short discussion of bridging research to practice.

Measuring Outcomes in Efficacy and Effectiveness Trials

By the time you reach Steps 3 and 4 of the intervention research process, you have a program theory, which specifies activities, mediators or targets for change, and expected outcomes. At this step, you also have either a logic model or a theory of change (see Chapter 3) that maps the theoretical linkage between program activities and outcomes. In addition, your model or theory is the basis for a plan for measurement, including measuring the extent to which intervention activities occurred as intended. Measurement, reviewed in this section, is necessary to show covariation, which is one of the three conditions needed in making causal arguments.

Most intervention research begins with a focus on a *construct*. Constructs are concepts that are not readily observable. Constructs include health, delinquency, depression, well-being, child neglect, and other phenomena that are social, psychological, and—in some cases—legal constructions. For measurement, constructs require operationalization, which is the process of defining a construct in terms that can be observed. We seek measures that have the quality of being *reliable* (i.e., repeatable measurement yields the same result) and *valid* (i.e., the measured value relates well to the true value of the construct). For example, if our intervention is intended to impact health and well-being, we have to define how we are going to measure the constructs of health and well-being. We might choose to ask participants to indicate whether they feel the intervention positively or negatively affected their health and well-being. But such reports are highly subjective (though self-report can be valid) and might lack reliability. Reliable instruments (those that get similar results with repeated measurement) generally include a series of related questions that indicate different aspects of a construct. Therefore, we might define health as a score from a standardized health assessment inventory such as RAND Corporation's SF-36 (2008). In the case of other constructs, we might use self-reports of illegal behavior as an indicator of delinquency, or use the *Diagnostic and Statistical Manual of Mental Disorders* to operationalize depression as a specific configuration of behavior (American Psychiatric

Construct	An idea or theoretical construction (sometimes called a factor)
Measurement	The process of selecting instruments, refining survey questions, confirming scales, and other data collection procedures designed to measure constructs
Variable	A measurable indicator

Figure 5.2 Conceptual hierarchy of measurement.

Association 2000). Illustrated in Figure 5.2, measurement is the process of linking theoretical constructs to observable indicators.

One strategy should predominate in measurement: central constructs should be measured in more than one way (see McDavid and Hawthorn 2006; Trochim 2005). The goal of measurement is to derive several alternative ways to represent important concepts. Some ways of accomplishing this goal include using more than one instrument, using different reporters (e.g., parent, child, and teacher reports), or using different methods of data collection (e.g., both quantitative and qualitative, or behavioral observation and self-report).

Qualitative measurement approaches (e.g., in-depth interviewing, focus groups, and thematic analysis) are especially useful for pilot studies where program components are being formulated and revised. And in efficacy and effectiveness studies, they are particularly valuable in describing the quality of program implementation. Qualitative methods complement quantitative methods. Transcribing recorded interviews with program participants provides word-for-word text, which can be analyzed and applied to understanding the relation of intervention processes to outcomes.

Quantitative measures and qualitative methods should be pilot tested. Measures should be logically correlated with other similar variables. That is, they should have *concurrent validity* and have a pattern of relationships that makes sense. For example, one measure of delinquency should be correlated with other measures of delinquency. In addition, measures should be culturally sensitive, easily understood by respondents, and conceptually congruent with program theory. Cultural constructions of words and phrases can differ by region, age, class, race/ethnicity, national origin, and a variety of other factors. The language of instruments should be pilot tested to make sure that meanings are clear (Do program participants understand "sneakers" to mean the same thing as "tennis shoes"? Do they think "feeling blue" is more or less serious than "feeling depressed"?). As we discussed in Chapter 4, cultural nuances in meaning often reflect different social constructions of common constructs like "good parenting" or "healthy body image." Pilot tests can include talking to potential program participants about how they interpret or understand the questions included in the instruments. Of course, to correlate any explanatory variable with culture requires a reliable indicator of the "culture" construct. Researchers often use demographic indicators of race, ethnic group, place of birth, and preferred language as proxies for culture. However, the research literature also includes scales of culture and acculturation that are potentially valuable during pilot tests (Escobar and Vega 2000; Marin *et al.* 1987).

Measurement of Fidelity in Efficacy and Effectiveness Trials

The purpose of measuring the implementation of an intervention is to determine whether it was delivered with fidelity. A well-conceived program that cannot be implemented with fidelity will have no reliable effect. Indeed, a poorly implemented program should not be evaluated because it is not possible to describe what caused outcomes (if there are any). In this section, we discuss implementation fidelity in the context of the logic of experimentation. We address why researchers measure the quantity and quality of program implementation, and how to construct measures of implementation to indicate faithful use of a program model.

As noted previously, *implementation* refers to the delivery of an intervention program. Programs provided with high fidelity are consistent with program theory. How well or how poorly an intervention is implemented is influenced by *implementation drivers*, factors that affect the fidelity of a program (Fixsen, Naoom, Blasé, Friendman, and Wallace 2005). Implementation drivers include many factors such as the recruitment of qualified intervention agents (e.g., practitioners) and the training, coaching, and support they receive from supervisors and administrators. In addition, the concept of drivers takes account of environmental factors that affect implementation. These include the climate and culture of the organization in which an intervention is delivered.

Fidelity and the Stages of Intervention Research

In the context of the intervention research process, the central difference between efficacy and effectiveness trials is that the researcher in an efficacy trial uses a variety of means to *induce successful implementation* (Shadish *et al.* 2002), which is a big undertaking. The researcher wishes to control (and support) as much of the intervention process as possible and thereby ensure that the program is implemented as intended. In contrast, the researcher in an effectiveness trial sets the implementation of the program in motion and, though consultation and assistance may be available on request, tends to let routine agency practices influence fidelity.

Fidelity links the implementation of an intervention to outcomes; it is defined by the extent to which a program follows an intended program model. Establishing criteria for the successful implementation of a program—sometimes called fidelity criteria—is critical to the successful dissemination of evidence-based interventions. Not surprisingly, numerous studies have found that program effectiveness is related to fidelity (e.g., Elliott and Mihalic 2004). Increasingly, agencies have turned to fidelity measures as a way to monitor program implementation and provide real-time feedback to practitioners. In this sense, measures of fidelity are used both to guide concurrent implementation and to provide a means of quality assurance. For researchers, fidelity criteria indicate whether an intervention was sufficiently implemented to warrant a test of its efficacy or effectiveness. Fidelity measurement should provide a clear program description in terms of (1) the intensity and quality of the procedures used, and (2) how those procedures differed from the experience of participants in the control or comparison conditions. Coupled with an intervention manual, measurable fidelity criteria aid in program replication by providing information about the dosage of the program, its frequency, intensity, and duration of services. Often, researchers use fidelity criteria to identify failures to implement and sometimes to account for negative findings. In the next section, we describe the four main functions of fidelity measurement.

Fidelity Measurement Ensures Model Adherence in Evaluation

The most common use of fidelity measures is to determine whether a program was delivered as specified by program theory. In estimating program effects, program measurement can detect two types of fidelity-related problems: low treatment fidelity in which fidelity is low in the intervention group, and compromised fidelity in which the comparison group evidences intervention content, whether by inadvertent treatment diffusion or some other reason. This potential for error leads to the rule of thumb in intervention research: *The treatment must be measured both in intervention groups and non-intervention groups.* Bond and colleagues argued, "it is important to examine the implementation of both experimental and control groups along the same study dimensions in order to determine the degree of treatment differentiation, which is the systematic variance that is expected to account for any differences in outcomes" (Bond, Evans, Salyers, Williams, and Kim 2000, 78). For example, as a classroom-based social development intervention, *Making Choices* was provided in an effectiveness trial by third-grade teachers in a treatment condition, whereas teachers in a comparison group used their existing curricula. A questionnaire was given to teachers in both groups to measure their use of social development activities. Although almost all of the teachers in the treatment group reported teaching social development lessons on a weekly basis (indicating high "model integrity" for *Making Choices*), a significant percentage of the teachers in the comparison group also reported weekly instruction using social development activities. This presence of intervention-related content in the control condition (i.e., low "model differentiation") led to a reconceptualization of the study. Instead of a comparison between classes with and without social development lessons, we discovered we had a study comparing manualized research-based lessons to informal teacher-initiated lessons on social development.

Fidelity Measurement Provides a Precise Summary
of Program Expectations

In a roundabout way, the process of developing fidelity criteria also contributes to program theory and formulation. Fidelity measurement instruments themselves can be helpful in establishing the operational definition of program activities. Even when program materials, guidelines, and manuals are fully developed, fidelity measures can serve as a summary of precisely what is expected to occur. They succinctly specify essential content.

Fidelity Measures Contribute to Meta-Analyses

In addition, reporting on fidelity in the literature can be a key element for meta-analyses across similar interventions. In meta-analysis, studies and programs are grouped, in part, according to the level of implementation. When valid fidelity measures are developed, they contribute to cross-study analyses based on differential implementation.

Fidelity Measures Identify "Active" Ingredients in
Program Models

Finally, fidelity measures can be used in efficacy studies to establish thresholds for program exposure. They can help specify various components of the program package, and they aid in identifying the core ingredients of interventions. They provide a basis for determining whether program components were implemented with sufficient rigor to permit mediation analyses, and they are the basis for efficacy subset analyses where outcomes are compared for participants who receive differing amounts of the experimental program.

Developing Measures of Fidelity

Fidelity measures are developed in two stages. First, fidelity criteria for an intervention must be articulated based on program theory and prior research. This process usually involves describing the program elements that distinguish an experimental intervention from routine services.

Second, measures of implementation are developed from fidelity criteria. These measures indicate whether program providers behave similarly to one another, focus on the same goals, and have comparable levels of effort. Measures of implementation should distinguish intervention activities from activities in control or comparison groups.

Developing Fidelity Criteria

Mowbray and her colleagues (2003) searched the mental and general health, education, and social services literature for descriptions of fidelity criteria and measures. They found that fidelity criteria were typically drawn from three sources: (1) a specific program model including an articulated theory of change, program materials, and related literature; (2) expert opinions of what the critical criteria for a program ought to be; and (3) qualitative research involving practitioners or other stakeholders who have high program familiarity. Criteria should differentiate the essential components of an intervention from activities that are not required or part of the intervention.

From program theory, specified mediators should guide the selection of fidelity criteria. Often the data can be helpful in identifying fidelity criteria. For example, results from our early tests of *Making Choices* indicated that students in classrooms that completed the program manual and received more than 17.5 hours of intervention exposure (i.e., *Making Choices* lessons) had significantly better outcomes. Therefore, the data provided a benchmark for a structural measure of fidelity: completion of the program *and* a minimum of 17.5 hours of program activities.

Fidelity criteria should include both prescribed and proscribed activities (Bond *et al.* 2000). It is curious to think of a program description that includes proscribed activities, isn't it? However, the evidence base is becoming sufficiently strong to identify activities that may produce harm. For instance, *Making Choices* has research support as a regular education classroom intervention, but it has not been tested with small homogeneous groups of students who are referred for aggressive behavior problems—the kinds of groups you might find if only students with aggressive behavior were selected out of their classrooms. Therefore, *Making Choices* program materials direct practitioners to deliver the program to whole classrooms (or to other kinds of heterogeneously configured groups). Selecting aggressive children and placing them in groups is a proscribed activity. Indeed, it is inconsistent with the philosophy of *Making Choices* and the research literature suggests that grouping aggressive children may create opportunities for deviancy training (Dishion *et al.* 1999). Although it may be possible to conduct interventions in groups selected for a particular risk factor, such as aggressive behavior, this issue remains in contention in the literature. Thus, including criteria for not only how the intervention should be implemented, but also how the intervention should *not* be used is important to program fidelity.

Constructing Fidelity Rating Scales

A multimethod, multi-source process is used for measuring fidelity criteria. We often develop two types of instruments: (1) ratings of fidelity that are made by program experts based on their systematic observations, interviews with intervention agents or participants, program reports, and records; and (2) self-reports by intervention agents and program participants that indicate which program activities were completed (Bond *et al.* 2000). Measures of program *structure* relate to the duration and intensity of service delivery. These measures are often quantified as hours of program exposure. Program exposure can be conceptualized in a variety of ways: the number of program sessions, the length of sessions, or the number of prescribed activities covered in each session.

Measures of the *process* of program implementation relate to the way in which services are delivered. In contrast to quantity of program (i.e., measures of structure), process measures focus on the quality of the service. Process measures involve the use of prescribed program principles, levels of participant engagement, and quality assessment of program activities. In the evaluation of *Making Choices,* our measure of structure-related fidelity factors relied on practitioner self-reports that included the amount of time spent providing the lessons and the specific activities covered in each lesson. For process-related factors, a classroom observer sat in while the teacher delivered a *Making Choices* lesson. Using an observational rating form, the classroom observer reported on how well the teacher established classroom rules, used behavior feedback and redirect techniques, implemented a variety of behavior-management tools, followed instructional protocols, showed skillful communication with students, and demonstrated intentional use of groups and social dynamics. In addition to these observations, more fidelity-process data were collected through teacher interviews conducted throughout the school year as well as after program completion.

Measuring Fidelity in Practice: Multisystemic Therapy

Multisystemic therapy (MST) is a well-researched, family-centered intervention designed to treat antisocial behavior in adolescents (Halliday-Boykins and Henggeler 2001; Littell 2005; Rowland, Halliday-Boykins, Henggeler, Cunningham, Lee, Kruesi, and Shapiro 2005; Sundell, Hansson, Lefhölm, Olsson, Gustle, and Kadesjö 2008; Timmons-Mitchell, Bender, Kishna, and Mitchell, 2006). MST represents an exception to most of the interventions we have discussed in this text because it is not fully manualized and prescribed. Because the techniques in this intervention are too complex for step-by-step guides, MST protocols are based on nine practice principles that guide practitioners in formulating intervention plans. To support the fidelity of the program during implementation, the founder of MST Scott Henggeler and his colleagues created an extensive training and quality-assurance package that includes a set of manuals for organizations implementing MST, for therapists working with youth, and for clinical consultants who coach teams of MST therapists. In addition, consultation, training, and clinical supervision are provided to MST therapists with the goal of maintaining high levels of fidelity with prescribed program principles.

To measure implementation fidelity, MST researchers developed evaluation and feedback measures for the range of stakeholders in MST (i.e., practitioners, clinical supervisors, consultants, and participating families). Qualitative reports of MST implementation are provided by the practitioners during their weekly supervision sessions, and expert consultants (who function as an extension of the MST development team) collect data from both the clinical supervisors and the therapists.

Quantitative measures of implementation fidelity are collected using the Therapist Adherence Measure (TAM), which the MST research group developed as a questionnaire for participating families. Comprised of 15 items, the TAM provides information on the practitioners' adherence to MST principles (Henggeler and Borduin, 1992). In addition, MST researchers developed a Consultant Adherence Measure (CAM), in which MST practitioners record the performance of their consultants. In randomized trials, TAM surveys completed by caregivers showed that high therapist fidelity to MST predicted positive therapeutic outcomes, such as improved family functioning, reduced arrest rates, and fewer out-of-home placements. The CAM has 44 items that fall into three sub-scales: perceived consultant competence, consultant alliance with the therapist, and MST procedures (Schoenwald, Sheidow, and Letourneau 2004). Schoenwald and her colleagues hypothesized that CAM and TAM measures would be correlated with outcomes. They found this to be true when, and only when, the consultant scored high on the competence scale. Surprisingly, consultant alliance with the therapist predicted less adherence to MST principles by the therapist (i.e., lower fidelity) and negative child outcomes. These findings alerted the program developers that consultant alliance by itself, in the absence of fidelity to the program model, was not sufficient to produce desired outcomes.

In this example, intervention researchers based their fidelity criteria on a well-articulated program theory and quality-assurance support protocol. They developed measures to collect both quantitative and qualitative data from all the stakeholders. Exemplary in the field of social intervention, Henggeler and his colleagues' approach demonstrates the utility of fidelity measures in illuminating the black box called treatment. Measurement of fidelity led to a more nuanced and even unexpected understanding of intervention processes.

Bridging Efficacy and Effectiveness Trials: The Research to Practice Challenge

The logic of intervention research calls for a sequence of trials to develop a program in pilot testing, to refine and confirm program components through efficacy studies, and then to test program effectiveness in practice venues. A sequence of studies is necessary because efficacy is necessary but not sufficient for effectiveness (Flay 1986). So why not skip the efficacy test and just run the effectiveness trial? Without first establishing a program's efficacy, negative findings in an effectiveness trial are hard to interpret—they may be the result of a failure of the program model or of a failure to implement the program with fidelity.

A case can be made, however, that efficacy and effectiveness testing should be blended to strengthen the chances that proven programs will—right out of the box—be more congruent with real world practice. Glasgow, Lichtenstein, and Marcus (2003) argued that the failure of many efficacy trials to address environmental and organizational factors has resulted in a backlog of "promising" programs that appear efficacious in carefully controlled conditions, but are not well suited for practice environments. This is due, in part, to the way efficacy trials are conceptualized. Efficacy trials are purposefully designed to maximize impact, and therefore they often control factors that can disrupt treatment delivery, receipt, and adherence. As we have discussed in this chapter, this control is accomplished by a variety of means. Guided by carefully developed program theories, research teams are selective about the participants recruited for studies. For example, researchers may exclude potential participants with co-occurring conditions or participants with histories of prior service failures. Researchers sometimes pay participants for participation or their interventions have cash transfer features (see the Progresa Study in Chapter 7) that may affect outcomes. Sometimes interventions have multiple elements that all make sense in terms of prior research, but together are just far too complicated to be widely adopted. For example, even though some multielement delinquency prevention programs have been shown to be effective, these programs require schools to provide in-home family services; this requires providing an intervention in a way that most school districts have neither the policy mandate nor resources (e.g., skilled staff) to implement (see Prochaska, Evers, Prochaska, Van Marter, and Johnson 2007).

From our perspective, if the goal of intervention research is to strengthen the connection between research and practice, then efficacy trials also must be conducted in practice settings. Though scaled down, such agency-based efficacy trials need to have characteristics that are similar to effectiveness trials. They should attend to the socioorganizational culture and climate factors that affect the adoption and maintenance of interventions in practice. These blended trials should be consistent with public policies, practice guidelines, state and local codes, and with reimbursement schema. Carrying out efficacy trials in practice settings is perhaps the best way to address the gap between the number of programs that perform well in small lab- or clinic-based trials and the number of programs that subsequently perform poorly in community settings. As a part of program design and development, we must assess the expected reach of a program under routine agency conditions. We address this issue in the next chapter.

Additional Reading

For a detailed discussion of the sequence of trials approach to intervention research see Flay (1986), and for a critical response describing some of the shortcomings of a strictly sequenced approach, see Glasgow *et al.* (2003).

Flay, Brian R. (1986). Efficacy and effectiveness trials (and other phases of research) in the development of health promotion programs. *Preventive Medicine, 15*(5): 451–474.

Glasgow, Russell E., Edward Lichtenstein, and Alfred C. Marcus. (2003). Why don't we see more translation of health promotion research to practice? Rethinking the efficacy-to-effectiveness transition. *American Journal of Public Health, 93*(8): 1261–1267.

The following texts are recommended for their coverage of issued related to research methods and design:

Rossi, Peter H., Mark W. Lipsey, and Howard E. Freeman. (2003). *Evaluation: A systematic approach.* 7th ed. Thousand Oaks, CA: Sage.

Shadish, William R., Thomas D. Cook, and Donald T. Campbell. (2002). *Experimental and quasi-experimental designs for generalized causal inference.* New York: Houghton Mifflin.

Trochim, William, M. K. (2005). *Research methods: The concise knowledge base.* Cincinnati, OH: Atomic Dog.

6

Step 5: Dissemination of Findings and Program Materials: The Challenge of Evidence-Based Practice

---

The Challenge of Evidence-Based Practice

This book is about change—it is about designing change strategies based on research, and evaluating those change strategies in practice. We contend that good practice and good research are excellent partners because, when practice is informed by research, outcomes are often improved. Likewise, when research is informed by practice, the programs that are developed are likely a better fit for the intended population and the intended setting. For well over 100 years, scholars have been working to improve the scientific bases for social-health services—the benefits of those efforts are now emerging.

However, whether focused on the etiology of social and health problems or the effectiveness of the services designed to address problems, the translation of scientific information to practice has rarely operated as intended. Early research findings were often equivocal and interventions were poorly defined; even when interventions seemed to work, they were black boxes with no clear explanation of why they were successful. Fortunately, this situation has begun to change as researchers have based interventions on specific mechanisms hypothesized to mediate risk and outcomes, resulting in more focused interventions and a growing body of promising findings.

Despite these advances, the transfer of knowledge to practice has remained painfully slow. Indeed, the practice strategies employed by current health and mental health professionals may be lagging behind research knowledge by as much as 15 or 20 years (Brekke, Ell, and Palinkas 2007; Institute of Medicine 2001). To close this gap, we need to give greater consideration to dissemination and diffusion in intervention research. As a new program progresses from early design to pilot testing, and then through efficacy and effectiveness trials, we need to anticipate the contingencies that will influence its adoption in the real world. Brekke and colleagues conceptualized this dissemination planning in two phases:

> Phase I includes moving knowledge from basic science to more applied usage in human studies including efficacy and effectiveness trials of clinical intervention. Phase 2 translation concerns research aimed at enhancing the adoption of best practices to the community. (2007, 123).

Evidence-Based Practice Integrates Research Findings with Clinical Judgment

The uptake of research knowledge into routine practice has been accelerated by the evidence-based practice movement. Evidence-based practice (EBP) began in medicine, but it was quickly adopted by other health and allied health professions. Furthermore, a report from a National Institute of Mental Health Symposium on the Integration of Research and Practice in Mental Health makes a distinction between evidence-based treatment (EBT) and EBP (Institute for the Advancement of Social Work Research, 2007). This distinction holds that EBTs are those practices that have been subjected to repeated rigorous scientific research and have been shown to be effective with a particular population.

In contrast, EBP refers to an explicit process for making practice-related decisions based on the best currently available evidence. Shown in Figure 6.1, EBP involves considering a range of factors in making practice decisions, including EBT, other research, client preference, practice circumstances, and the practitioner's expertise and experience (Haynes, Devereaux, and Guyatt 2002). Figure 6.1 depicts the complex interaction that ensues under EBP. This model is applicable at the individual, family, group, organization, and community levels of intervention. Practitioners first review the problem and circumstances presented by the client (including environmental supports and constraints) and the strengths that the client brings to the situation. At the same time, practitioners must explore and clarify client preferences and needs. The client's perspective regarding problem formulation and preferences regarding intervention planning is a crucial element of EBP. These first two sections of the EBP model set the stage for the practitioner to access the research through appropriate databases, which pertain specifically to the issues that have been raised.

Figure 6.1. Model for evidence-based practice decisions. Source: Haynes, Brian, Deveraux, and Guyatt 2002, 38–38. Used with permission.

Mutually formulated by the practitioner and client, the problem guides the search for and selection of an EBT. The practitioner may find a number of potential EBTs that are appropriate for the issue and the client, but it is also possible that the practitioner will find no clearly established and preferred EBT. Furthermore, even if there are appropriate EBTs, they may not be available for use because they are too expensive, too complex, or simply out of reach. What should be done then? Recall that EBP relies on the best available current evidence. This is a nearest neighbor strategy, in which practitioners are ethically obligated to identify the best *available* intervention strategy. The availability of an EBT is determined by agency policies, the cost of an EBT, and—perhaps most important—whether the practitioner has been or can be trained to provide that EBT. We believe that training, which is discussed later in this chapter, is a linchpin in the dissemination of EBTs.

All of this is conditioned on the practitioner's experience and general expertise. The practitioner's knowledge and skill are critical to the success of EBP in that the total process—including assessment, listening and responding to client preferences, as well as accessing and applying an EBT—must be implemented within a professional stance. It is professional expertise within the context of a carefully crafted relationship that fosters positive change. Thus, EBP defines a practice decision-making process that guides making intervention choices based on the available EBTs, practitioner expertise, and client preference (Sackett, Rosenberg, Gray, Haynes, and Richardson 1996). Implicitly, EBP includes attention to whether the knowledge accrued in the basic and applied sciences has been translated for practice and whether that translated knowledge—no matter how compellingly valid—is available for use.

Unfortunately, the more we learn about the use of EBP, the clearer it becomes that EBTs are penetrating real-world practice at an unacceptably slow rate (Fixsen *et al.* 2005; Glasgow *et al.* 2003). On balance, the best current EBTs are not available in practice. The School Success Profile (SSP) and its practice framework—assessment of individuals and schools using a newly designed assessment protocol followed by a choice of interventions gleaned from the EBT and EBP literature—were developed in a variety of elementary, middle, and high schools. The developers thought that because the SSP was regarded as useful, school-based practitioners would use the program; however, this was not the case. The lag in the uptake of the SSP is not atypical. The truth is that the diffusion of interventions to community practice is very difficult. Diffusion does not occur in the course of natural events. What the SSP researchers learned was that the uptake of evidence-based practices is largely about organizations and the sociopolitical context of practice. Aarons summed up this situation by explaining that "it is necessary to understand and consider attitudes towards adoption of EBP's [sic] of providers who are embedded within the complex organizational context of . . . service systems" (2004, 62).

Stages in the Implementation of Evidence-Based Programs

It is only in the past decade that the topic of translation and adaptation has risen to prominence as a serious practice problem. It is even more recent that major federal and foundation resources have been allocated to conduct research on this topic, including dissemination of program materials, implementation with fidelity, and adaptation to alternative contexts and cultures. These research efforts constitute a new field of endeavor—one from which we are likely to learn much in the coming years. At least provisionally, we can think of implementation at the program level as being comprised of five linked stages that lead from initial exploration of a potential program by possible users to its adoption and maintenance over time (Fixsen *et al.* 2005). According to Fixsen and colleagues (2005) these stages include (1) exploration and adoption, (2) program installation, (3) initial implementation, (4) full operation, and (5) sustainability. To avoid confusion with the five steps of intervention research or the four stages of manual development note that these five stages refer only to the process of implementing an already established intervention.

Stage 1: Exploration and Adoption

For exploration of adoption to occur, someone at an organization has to become aware of the availability of an innovation. A practitioner or an administrator may have read an article in a journal, attended a conference on research, talked to a colleague about new and available practice innovations, or reviewed an advertisement or promotional materials. This information usually precipitates an evaluative process. Before any program can be adopted for use by an organization, it must be assessed in terms of its fit with current practices and the cost of the product. Cost includes the purchase price, the cost of training, and opportunity costs vis-à-vis time required to implement. Approval by leaders at the top of the organizational hierarchy can be helpful. The SSP program developers found that if they could secure the endorsement of a district superintendent or school principal, the SSP had a greater chance of adoption.

Stage 2: Program Installation

Once the decision is made by an organization to implement a specific innovation, a program installation stage begins. Professional staff must be included in the implementation process, resources must be realigned, and practitioners have to be trained. Equally important, an organizational climate must be cultivated that is favorable toward the intervention effort and will sustain efforts over time. We have found that practitioners are often comfortable with "tried and true" methods of intervention and enticing them to experiment with a new program can be challenging. To overcome this challenge, experimentation with new methods must be accompanied by substantial training, supervision, collegial support, directive and responsive leadership, and organizational policies that reinforce the implementation process (Aarons 2004; Fixsen et al. 2005).

Stage 3: Initial Implementation

At this stage, the innovation has become integrated as part of the organization. Integration involves sustained organizational change in staffing patterns, behavioral expectations (e.g., required knowledge and skills for practitioners), and supervision (Fixsen et al. 2005). In the case of the SSP, the data obtained have to be explained to parents and students who work together with school personnel to identify issues to be addressed and potential interventions to be used. This open and inclusive involvement requires cooperation among professional staff and consumers.

The successful implementation of a new program is related to the fit of an intervention to the socioorganizational characteristics of the setting. Recent data suggest that organizational culture and climate are related directly to the implementation of evidence-based treatments (Glisson *et al.* 2008a, 2008b). *Organizational culture* is comprised of work expectations and the level of formalization. Poor program implementation is likely to occur in settings with rigid hierarchies and low expectations for proficiency. *Organizational climate* is comprised of psychological constructs, such as workplace stress, peer cooperation, and emphasis on personal achievement. Settings with high stress, low cooperation, and weak rewards for performance are unlikely to deliver an intervention with fidelity. Because the features of the setting are less well controlled in effectiveness trials, treatment delivery is likely to be affected by the setting climate and culture. This suggests that to promote dissemination we must consider the demand characteristics of interventions on the social structures and processes operating within the organizations in which we expect implementation to occur.

Stage 4: Full Operation

In Stage 4 of dissemination and adoption, the intervention is no longer considered an innovation. The program is understood as normative within an organization and integrated into the sociopolitical context (Fixsen *et al.* 2005). In the full operation of the SSP, practitioners, students, and families come to see the administration of the SSP as "business as usual."

Stage 5: Sustainability—Fidelity versus Local Adaptation?

Once in full operation, a new program must be sustained with fidelity. However, after the program has been in place and has become well integrated into the routine, staff may be tempted to alter it. Changes may occur because new staff members are untrained or receive less training than those involved with the initial implementation, some staff members may be uncommitted to the program, or some may desire to improve results or strengthen the fit of a program with organizational contingencies, community mores and wishes, and public policies. When program changes of this nature occur, it is sometimes called *program drift*. However, when program changes occur because practitioners purposively modify an EBT to improve fit with local practice conditions, it is called *local adaptation*.

There is often tension between fidelity and local adaptation (Elliott and Mihalic 2004). This raises an important question: Once an intervention is fully implemented, should local practitioners adapt it to respond to the specific community, clientele, or environment? On the one hand, we may have evidence from research that the intervention—as initially conceived and implemented by the developers—produces predictable results. On the other hand, professionals in the field may come to the conclusion that alterations in the intervention will produce more positive outcomes. These practitioners often have great expertise and extensive knowledge of the population and setting. Thus, local adaptations may be valuable and point to unaddressed problem areas and significant implementation issues. However, these local changes can also compromise a program's effectiveness. Indeed, because the changes are untested they may be at odds with the process of EBP. Sustainability presents challenges in counterbalancing fidelity with local adaptation. Elliott and Mihalic argue that: "The available research demonstrates that fidelity is related to effectiveness and any bargaining away of fidelity will most likely decrease program effectiveness" (2004, 51).

Cultural Adaptation to Promote Relevance and Reach

Given tension between fidelity and local adaptation, it is no wonder that the cultural adaptation of EBTs is a matter of much discussion. Differences between the population for which an EBT was originally developed and the population for which an EBT may be adopted often occur and can constitute a barrier to the reach and relevance of a program. Adapting a program may improve its appeal and, when it is delivered, increase the adherence of participants to program protocols. For example, on a general level, adaptation may hold the potential to reduce health disparities in the availability of EBTs to relevant racial and ethnic groups. Given the fact that currently in the United States, 25% of the population experiences significant disparities in the availability of health care and that these disparities increase disease rates (e.g., cancer, diabetes, substance abuse, heart disease) and result in a reduced life expectancy, program adaptation to improve cultural relevancy and to enhance health outcomes is of great national importance (National Institutes of Health 2006). Critics, however, argue for limits on the number and range of adaptations. The critics who offer this caution charge that haphazard adaptation usually compromises program processes, and that we usually have no reliable data on which to base changes in program content and processes (Lau 2006).

Because of the diverse demography of the United States and the desirability of extending the reach of EBTs to other countries and cultures, the dissemination of EBTs will inevitably involve delivering a program to a population for which we have no or little evidence of program effectiveness (i.e., a population on which the program has not been tested). In this circumstance, two kinds of adaptation seem warranted. The first is adaptation to improve compatibility with organizational contingencies (Weisz, Jensen, and McLeod 2005). This type of adaptation is best done at the point when the program is first adopted, and best carried out by a group of administrative and program experts who understand the service system and the population it serves. The second kind of adaptation involves tailoring a program to improve its cultural congruence. Both kinds of adaptation are systematic and should be guided by the best available evidence. Both types of adaptation should result in EBTs that are not only a better fit with the context but also more flexible in providing options for adjusting content to improve appeal without compromising efficacy.

Maintaining that balance between adaptation and fidelity is a challenging task because it requires a thorough understanding of the social or health problem, the program theory that is the basis of an EBT, and the mediational mechanisms that operate in the target community. If we adopt this perspective, there are at least two situations in which adaptation appears warranted (Lau 2006). First, *adaptation is warranted when risk and protective factors are known to vary by culture.* In particular, knowledge of protective processes that are culturally specific may serve as bases for improving theories of change related to EBTs. For example, we have compelling evidence that strong family ties buffer Latino children from adversity during immigration. Thus, when a proven parenting program is provided in Latino communities, the program could be adapted by adding content on *familism*, which is the Latin concept of family interests taking precedence over individual interests (Bacallao and Smokowski 2005). Second, *adaptation is warranted when a community perceives an intervention as having low social validity.* That is, when the intended target group does not find a proposed intervention meaningful or useful and thus declines to engage in the program. There are many factors affecting rates of participation, and these factors vary across racial and ethnic groups, including the acceptability of specific treatment modalities, mistrust of systems, and stigma related to different kinds of interventions. When program experts know that the reach and engagement of an EBT are likely to be negatively affected by community views, adaptation is warranted. Adaptation may involve reframing the understanding of the intervention so that unfavorably perceived elements are viewed in a more favorable light. Of course, the challenge is to improve cultural appeal without sacrificing or misrepresenting valid program elements.

Does Cultural Adaptation Improve Effectiveness?

The adaptations discussed above focus largely on improving contextual fit and cultural congruence to strengthen reach, recruitment, and retention. Are there circumstances when an intervention might be adapted to expand efficacy? Although this is certainly controversial, the answer seems to be positive. One example comes from the adaptation of a parenting training program that had been developed based on a series of studies involving European American, non-Latino families. Working as a team, staff at the Oregon Social Learning Center (OSLC) and community members undertook a review process to adapt the program for Latino immigrant families in Oregon. They systematically reviewed the program for conceptual-theoretical relevance (e.g., Is the concept of positive reinforcement for prosocial behavior relevant and appropriate for Latino families?) and operational relevance (e.g., Is the way we teach parents culturally sensitive and relevant?). The team developed new content to address culturally specific risk and protective factors, and they presented an adapted program to focus groups of Latino parents who provided feedback on program strategies, terminology, and delivery. From these groups, it was decided, for example, to call intervention agents *entrenadores* (coaches), and a theme of parent empowerment was woven through program content. Emphasis on empowerment was seen as reinforcing the traditional role of parents but also as providing support during acculturation, when many parents feel distanced from their children who tend to learn English and develop non-Latino friends more rapidly. The adapted parenting program was shown to produce effect sizes comparable to the effect sizes observed in the original studies of the parenting training program, which did not include Latino participants (Martinez and Eddy 2005). A nascent evidence base suggests that careful, research-informed adaptation may improve not only reach and retention but it may also affect efficacy.

Shown in Figure 6.2, cultural adaptation to extend efficacy is warranted when the evidence base for an intervention suggests that a problem has both broadly relevant and culturally or contextually distinct risk and protective processes and outcomes (Barrera and Castro 2006). When a problem is affected by both kinds of processes, each should inform the selection of an EBT and, as shown in Figure 6.2, may inform the content of the intervention. This framework distinguishes risk processes that are common across cultures (or contexts) from those that are related to specific cultures, subgroups, or communities. When the evidence for culturally or contextually distinct processes is strong, not only may usual or expected outcomes be suppressed if culturally distinct risk and protective processes are not addressed but other related outcomes of high cultural relevance may go unrecognized and unmeasured.

As in the OSLC study, efficacy is potentially expanded if culturally specific risk and protective processes and outcomes are addressed. In an example used by Barrera and Castro (2006), an EBT for depression was

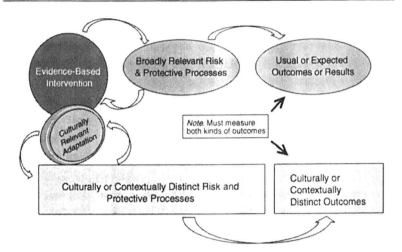

Figure 6.2. A conceptual framework for the adaptation of evidence-based interventions.

to be adapted for a Latino population. Research data suggested that common risk processes, such as those related to parental support and family communication, operate as well for potential Latino program participants (e.g., *familism*—which places interests, values, and demands of the family over individual interests, values, or demands—was consistent with the depression EBT). In addition, the data suggested that a unique risk process may operate through the stress associated with immigration. In this example, a culturally specific program element was developed to address the culturally specific mediator of immigration stress. Immigration stress was conceptualized as a mediator affecting the intended program outcome, depression; however, immigration stress was also conceptualized as affecting a culturally distinct program outcome, *immigration distress*. From this perspective, the efficacy of an EBT is potentially expanded by considering both culturally distinct risk and protective processes and, as noted in Figure 6.2, outcome measures related to these processes.

Other Kinds of Adaptations

Program adaptation to improve cultural congruence is a field of great interest within intervention research. What is more, work in this area is likely to inform other kinds of adaptations as well. If we use the emerging view that adaptation is justified when the evidence for other mediational mechanisms is strong (i.e., moderated mediation based on culture, race, or ethnicity), then it is conceivable to initiate adaptation based on other potential moderators such as social class, occupation, and density of neighborhoods. In some communities, these moderators may represent alternative mediational pathways and present new opportunities for program adaptation.

However, adaptation is controversial because, at least in part, the evidence on which it must be based is often weak. When adaptation is done properly, it is a systematic process that involves program and problem experts who consider the organizational and community context, the problem-related research, and culturally relevant theories of change. In addition, adaptation that is carried out properly can strengthen efficacy, and it should improve the reach, effectiveness, adoption, implementation, and maintenance of an EBT in practice (Jilcott, Ammerman, Sommers, and Glasgow 2007).

The adoption of a program as part of a routine practice can be seen as a process of exploration, experimentation, and integration into the functioning of an agency. A new intervention must pass informal tests of application by practitioners, clients, and others as it is diffused and implemented. Indeed, it is these rarely discussed and poorly understood informal tests or criteria that may prevent the implementation and adoption of many research-based programs.

Factors Influencing Program Implementation and Adoption:
Five Criteria for Diffusion

We have discussed five stages in the implementation of evidence-based programs and several issues regarding the cultural adaptation of programs.

As we think about the uptake of a program, it is clear that the factors affecting the ultimate fate of an intervention are only weakly linked to the research evidence. These factors include those that influence whether a program will be fully implemented and sustained over time, and factors that influence whether a program will be diffused successfully from research to practice. In other words, factors affecting a program's diffusion are not related to the elegance of the program theory, the size of observed treatment effects in efficacy trials, the sophistication of mediational analyses, or the quality of the journals that publish the findings. Often, the factors determining the ultimate fate of an intervention relate directly to the organizational and environmental context of practice. Perhaps this phenomenon explains the disparity between research knowledge and real-world practice. According to E. M. Rogers (1995), a new intervention must satisfy five practical criteria before it is likely to be implemented and sustained in practice. As noted in Chapter two, for successful diffusion a new intervention must be:

1. superior to services as usual,
2. compatible with agency practices,
3. no more complex than existing services,
4. easy to try (and reject if it fails), and
5. likely to produce tangible results recognizable by authorities as important.

Because the purpose of developing new programs is to improve practice outcomes, widespread adoption of effective interventions is perhaps the penultimate objective of intervention research. Considering the stages in implementing EBTs and the challenges of cultural adaptation, new programs must meet (some or perhaps even all of) these five criteria.

Superior to Services as Usual

The first criterion, that a program be superior to services as usual, routinely receives much attention. Establishing a program's superiority is the criterion most closely linked to tests of program components under controlled conditions (efficacy trials) and broader tests under scale conditions (effectiveness trials), especially so when the trials use a treatment as usual (TAU) control condition. Indeed, Rogers (1995) argued that this criterion can be met only if comparison conditions in efficacy and effectiveness trials constitute services as usual. That is, rather than showing that program outcomes are better than a no-treatment condition, new programs must demonstrate outcomes that are an improvement over currently available services. To make this case, researchers must collect data about services as usual. We must understand routine services and the extent to which current services are similar or dissimilar to the experimental services. For example, in a recent study of the *Making Choices* program, we were surprised to find that a majority of teachers in a TAU control condition reported that they used content quite similar to our intervention materials. Teachers in the TAU were interested in helping children solve social problems, and they had sought out materials similar to *Making Choices*. So to meet the first test, instead of showing that *Making Choices* was superior to classroom content without social instruction, we would have to demonstrate that *Making Choices* was superior to "services as usual" that included regular social development instruction.

*Compatible with Agency Practices, No More Complex Than
Existing Services, and Easy to Try*

If a new program or service is to be adopted, it must be compatible with existing practices unless these practices are deemed ineffective. If a service requires attitudes and beliefs that contradict usual practices or if a program would conflict with accepted conventions, it is unlikely to be adopted. Practitioners are unlikely to adopt new interventions if they perceive that the new methods are inconsistent with their professional values, organizational practices, and understanding of the cultural, ethnic, racial, and community issues that affect practice.

In a similar vein, a proposed new intervention should be no more complex than programs in place. Adoption is much more likely to occur if an intervention does not require substantial retraining or major changes in organizational policies. The extent to which a new intervention is easily understood and reasonable to implement will enhance the chance of initial adoption. We return to this point later, because although some interventions are more complex, they hold such potential to improve practice that they warrant the special strategies that may be needed to promote uptake. In our view, we should not limit EBP to only those EBTs that have complexity comparable to TAU.

Last, interventions that are perceived as easy to try—and easy to reject, if necessary—are more likely to be tested. Interventions that require a substantial investment of time before the program can be implemented are more likely to be viewed as being too difficult and time-consuming to try and reject. That is, the general perception is that it is better to forego these programs altogether than to risk making the substantial investment of time while faced with the possibility of rejecting the program if it proves to be a poor fit. This is not to suggest that EBTs that require change cannot be implemented, only that dissemination will require greater effort and commitment. It is prudent to recognize and take this effort into account in advance.

In disseminating interventions, practical considerations weigh as much in the diffusion process as the strength of research findings. Data collected from practitioners regarding real-world considerations such as the ease of implementation or fit with current organizational structure may be useful in marketing an intervention. Marketing and training materials should include reports from stakeholders regarding training, materials used, demands and burdens, convenience of use, and end-user satisfaction. For example, agency administrators who have adopted new interventions may be asked to comment about the ease of use, the need to invest in new equipment or technology, and the implications for staff training and recruitment. These comments can be used in creating a dissemination plan that anticipates the challenges of diffusion.

Likely to Produce Tangible Results

Once implemented, an EBT must generate the desired results and these results must be measurable. How will a stakeholder know if positive results were achieved? How long should a practitioner expect to implement a new program before change will be recognized? These are difficult questions. Practitioners and other agency personnel should consider what results will define tangible success and have measures in place to track those changes. Interventions that provide guidance on measuring both mediators and outcomes are more likely to be adopted.

Roles of the Practitioner and Researcher in the Intervention Research Process

Intervention research is rooted in practice. To ensure that relevant practice problems are identified and context-sensitive interventions are developed, collaboration between practitioners and researchers is essential in all five steps of intervention research (Galinsky, Turnbull, Meglin, and Wilner 1993). It is to this topic of collaboration that we now turn. In Figure 6.3 we explicate the roles of researchers and practitioners at each step in intervention research.

Step 1. Specify a Problem and Develop a Program Theory

In this step, practitioners and the research team may work together to explain and define the problem or area of concern. Practitioners may identify a pressing problem and join together with researchers to clarify issues or act as consultants to an already defined problem. Practitioners bring an immediate understanding of the practice context, and a sense of the historical context, that is, whether specific interventions have resulted in success in the past. The researcher helps to identify and clarify the problem, reviews the literature, and uses databases to place the identified concern into a theoretical context that informs the development of program theory.

Step 2. Create and Revise Program Materials

In this step, the researcher collaborates with the practitioner to conceptualize intervention strategies and develop program materials that are rooted in a theory of change or logic model. The practitioner contributes knowledge and understanding of the agency setting, organizational constraints, policy limitations, local cultural factors, and community conditions affecting practice. Researchers often take primary responsibility for writing the program manual and materials, and integrating the best available research evidence into the program materials.

Step 3. Refine and Confirm Program Components

Step 3 begins the testing process in the community agency or another organization or field setting. In this step program materials are pilot

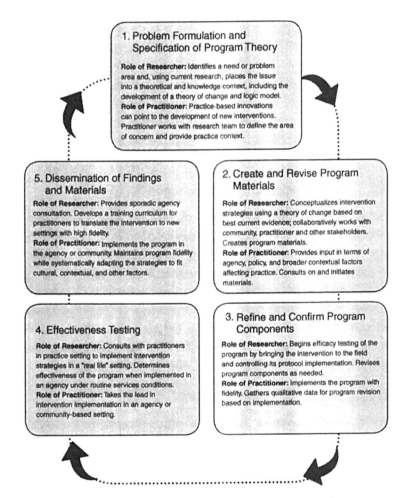

1. Problem Formulation and Specification of Program Theory

Role of Researcher: Identifies a need or problem area and, using current research, places the issue into a theoretical and knowledge context, including the development of a theory of change and logic model. **Role of Practitioner:** Practice-based innovations can point to the development of new interventions. Practitioner works with research team to define the area of concern and provide practice context.

5. Dissemination of Findings and Materials

Role of Researcher: Provides sporadic agency consultation. Develops a training curriculum for practitioners to translate the intervention to new settings with high fidelity. **Role of Practitioner:** Implements the program in the agency or community. Maintains program fidelity while systematically adapting the strategies to fit cultural, contextual, and other factors.

2. Create and Revise Program Materials

Role of Researcher: Conceptualizes intervention strategies using a theory of change based on best current evidence; collaboratively works with community, practitioner and other stakeholders. Creates program materials. **Role of Practitioner:** Provides input in terms of agency, policy, and broader contextual factors affecting practice. Consults on and initiates materials.

4. Effectiveness Testing

Role of Researcher: Consults with practitioners in practice setting to implement intervention strategies in a "real life" setting. Determines effectiveness of the program when implemented in an agency under routine services conditions. **Role of Practitioner:** Takes the lead in intervention implementation in an agency or community-based setting.

3. Refine and Confirm Program Components

Role of Researcher: Begins efficacy testing of the program by bringing the intervention to the field and controlling its protocol implementation. Revises program components as needed. **Role of Practitioner:** Implements the program with fidelity. Gathers qualitative data for program revision based on implementation.

Figure 6.3. Conceptualization of the steps of intervention research and data-driven practice collaboration.

tested and refined. Pilot testing of intervention components is often followed by small controlled trials. This is an iterative phase of research in which multiple studies may be conducted. The researcher is highly involved in overseeing the implementation and testing process and revising program components based on findings. Typically, practitioners implement the programs as designed and provide continuous feedback to the researcher about content, including aspects of a program that need to be revised. Collaboration between practitioners and researchers is critical in refining program materials and optimizing program effects. In this step a variety of resources and efforts are directed to the retention and continued compliance of study participants in attempts to optimize effect sizes. These include incentive payments to encourage study participation, provision of transportation to lessen the burden of participation, reinforcements for treatment adherence, and supervision by program developers to ensure compliance with program requirements.

Step 4. Assess the Effectiveness of Programs in a Variety of Settings and Circumstances

In Step 4, researchers function more as traditional program evaluators. They are less involved in the provision of the program, and they tend to be deeply involved in the collection and analysis of data. Feedback from practitioners continues to be a crucial element of the research process because implementation of program content in both experimental and control or comparison group conditions must be monitored. Although an intervention is not allowed to change during the course of an evaluation, qualitative data should be collected and used at the conclusion of the evaluation project to guide further refinement of the intervention.

Step 5. Disseminate Findings and Program Materials

In Step 5 of intervention research, we often think of practitioners as being responsible for the implementation of EBTs in such a way as to preserve the essential elements of programs that make them effective. Similarly, we usually think of program developers as continuing to refine training curricula, and those developers who are entrepreneurial may also develop training initiatives.

As we have discussed, dissemination is a complicated process. The gap between research and practice is affected by a variety of organizational factors, including inadequate time for professional development within agencies and work climates that do not support innovation and initiative (e.g., Henderson, MacKay, and Peterson-Badali 2006). It is becoming clear that the adoption of EBTs is not the sole responsibility of either the practitioner or the researcher. Indeed, adoption may be most influenced by state-level decisions regarding the kinds of services that may be funded under Medicaid or other programs, including private third-party payers in health-care organizations. Researchers have a responsibility to make their program materials available. Publishing houses have a responsibility to publish treatment manuals. Professional schools have a responsibility to teach EBTs. Professional organizations have a responsibility to advocate for the use of EBTs. Agencies have a responsibility to adopt EBTs and provide professional development related to EBTs. States have a responsibility to create public policies that support EBTs. All this points to a core problem: *There is no single infrastructure that bears responsibility for the dissemination and translation of EBTs.*

Research to Practice: Bridging the Gap

The dissemination of a practice innovation is a process involving the translation of research-based materials into practice-friendly protocols and the adaptation of research-based materials in ways that improve their fit with the practice setting, including the population served. Adaptation is a challenging process in which the core elements of EBTs must be identified and preserved. Adapting a program for a different setting or different population should be done by a team of people who are knowledgeable about both the new population with whom the program will be used and the program theory. In other words, the adaptation team must possess knowledge of the research on which the intervention is based, and that knowledge must be combined with practice experience. But adaptation and translation do not necessarily result in diffusion. Indeed, culturally appropriate materials on EBTs can be disseminated widely and yet not used by practitioners. Whose responsibility is it to ensure that EBTs are used in practice?

The fact is that no single person or organization has the capacity to oversee and ensure the adoption and use of EBTs. The diffusion of EBTs into practice must become a collective responsibility of state-level departments, local agencies, professional schools, and professional organizations. If the end goal is the adoption and sustained use of EBTs in practice, we need to bring to bear on this problem our knowledge of how people prepare to become practitioners. More often than not, this preparation includes professional training. In nearly all professions (trades may be different), knowledge and skill are developed conjointly in academic and practice settings. This model of training has roots in theories of learning, and it is used in medicine, nursing, psychology, public health, and social work. In social work, students learn through field placements that amount to about one-third of their professional training for the master's of social work degree. After graduation, professional training continues through workshops and professional development courses offered within agencies and by professional organizations. Hence, practice is a product of loosely connected systems of influence that are comprised of professional education, professional development, agency conditions and practices, and public policies and practice guidelines that broadly define services within service systems. Therefore, if we wish to change practice, we have to draw on knowledge related to how people learn and how systems change. Changing practice requires system-level interventions.

Many states have begun to recognize this problem, and in response they are beginning to develop new infrastructures to bridge the gap between research and practice. For example, the State of New York created an Evidence-Based Treatment Dissemination Center (EBTDC). Described in the text box, this center was initiated in 2005 and charged with the mission of improving the quality of clinical care for children and families in the state's mental health system (North *et al.* 2008). The development of the EBTDC was funded by a contract from the State Office of Mental Health to Columbia University, which developed a program based on research suggesting that educational exposure to EBTs and having self-efficacy in EBTs are predictors of adoption (Henderson *et al.* 2006). Center staff used a learning theory perspective to develop a dissemination intervention that included didactic content as well as ongoing reinforcement for implementation of EBTs. The goal of the EBTDC was daunting: to provide 400 social workers and other clinicians with training in EBTs in the course of one year. Though a formal evaluation has not been completed, the preliminary data suggest that the EBTDC was successful in training workers across New York in two EBTs—cognitive behavioral interventions for depression and for trauma.

The New York strategy was based on a RE-AIM perspective developed by Glasgow and his colleagues (2003). RE-AIM derives from the idea that different strategies are needed to promote the Reach, Efficacy, Adoption, Implementation, and Maintenance of proven interventions. Building *reach* involves understanding the setting and target population to present an EBT in a culturally engaging and contextually sensitive way. Strengthening *efficacy* involves using a stepped approach to incrementally build knowledge and provide for ongoing skill assessment with feedback. The EBTDC applied the stepped approach through offering an initial workshop that was followed up with group-based phone supervision. Promoting *adoption* involves showing that an EBT is superior to services as usual, compatible with existing agency practices, no more complex than existing services, easy to try (and reject if it fails), and likely to produce tangible, measurable results. As we discussed in Chapter 5, ensuring *implementation* requires establishing benchmarks for fidelity and putting in place a quality-assurance feedback system. Finally, guaranteeing the *maintenance* in practice of a proven intervention requires performance-based follow-up assessment, organizational incentives for implementation at benchmarks, and a policy environment in which reimbursements for EBTs are sufficient to support hiring and training qualified professionals.

Conclusion

Collaboration in training across and within systems is the linchpin of dissemination. Good ideas, quality research, sophisticated practice

Bridging Research and Practice:
The Evidence-Based Treatment Dissemination Center in New York

Funded by the State Office of Mental Health, New York's Evidence-Based Treatment Dissemination Center (EBTDC) at Columbia University was designed to train clinicians and supervisors who work with children and youth across the state. EBTDC staff developed training models for two evidence-based, cognitive behavioral interventions: one for depression and one for trauma (Office of Mental Health 2008). Training for each intervention was comprised of two phases: (a) a three-day workshop, and (b) one year of biweekly telephone consultation. In the workshop, the first day of training reviewed general content on EBTs and cognitive-behavioral interventions (e.g., cognitive techniques, psychoeducation, behavior activation, parent involvement, relapse prevention, and case assessment). The second and third days of the workshop training focused on specific EBTs and were led by program experts. Content on depression emphasized emotion-focused coping, cognitive restructuring, communications skills, and problem-solving skills. Content on trauma emphasized stress inoculation, relaxation, trauma narrative, gradual exposure, and cognitive processing.

The EBTDC project is based on the assumption that short training alone is insufficient to produce changes in practice (see, e.g., Bickman 1998); therefore, workshop participants were provided with biweekly, group-based phone consultation as follow-up to the workshop training events. Four doctoral-level clinicians led the calls, which averaged 90 minutes and followed a common format comprised of brief check-in and agenda setting, case presentation, round-robin case review, and discussion of program issues.

Overall, the EBTDC model of training is similar to models used in professional schools where academic content is presented and then followed by supervised practice. However, the EBTDC model is distinguished by its scope (an attempt to train more than 400 clinicians across an entire state), and its focus on two specific EBTs. In addition, the EBTDC model is distinguished by its group orientation in which clinician-participants share case information with other clinicians, telephone supervision is provided by program experts, and—perhaps axiomatic—leadership from the state's key mental health agency helped define the problem and organize a statewide effort to solve it.

The EBTDC research design is not sufficiently rigorous to assess the effect of the training. Nonetheless, from process data, it is known that about three-quarters (78.5%) of participants were social workers, and the vast majority (89.5%) of the participants worked in outpatient clinical settings.

(continued)

> Of the 417 clinicians who started the program, more than three-quarters (76%) completed the full year of follow-up phone consultation. On a five-point scale (1 = very negative; 5 = very positive) participant satisfaction levels averaged 4.1 for the cognitive-behavioral therapy overview day, 4.2 for the depression training day, and 4.4 for the day of trauma training. The data suggested that the program was well received by the clinician-participants. Although a controlled trial to determine the actual effect of the program on practice is needed, the findings are promising

knowledge, understanding of cultural nuances, and the best of intentions do not by themselves lead to fulfilling the RE-AIM framework. We consider collaboration as an exciting opportunity for research, administrative, and practice personnel to work together to develop and implement interventions like EBTDC that bridge the research to practice gap. This is the promise and the challenge of evidence-based practice.

Additional Reading

Brekke, John S., Kathleen Ell, and Lawrence Palinkas. (2007). Translational Science at the National Institute of Mental Health: Can Social Work Take Its Rightful Place? *Research on Social Work Practice, 17*(1): 123–133.

Elliott, Delbert S., and Sharon Mihalic (2004). Issues in disseminating and replicating effective prevention programs. *Prevention Science, 3*(1): 47–53.

Institute for the Advancement of Social Work Research. 2007. *Partnerships to integrate evidence-based mental health practices into social work education and research*. Retrieved on September 25, 2008 from http://www.charityadvantage.com/iaswr/EvidenceBasedPracticeFinal.pdf

Jilcott, Stephanie, Alice Ammerman, Janice Sommers, and Russell E. Glasgow. 2007. Applying the RE-AIM framework to assess the public health impact of policy change. *Annals of Behavioral Medicine, 34*(2): 105–114.

7

Challenges in Intervention Research

Previous chapters have emphasized synthesizing program theory from research, developing treatment manuals rooted in program theory, testing and refining program materials through a series of studies, and giving early consideration to fidelity and adaptation. We did not delve into the detail of research design or statistical methods because these topics are treated well in other texts (e.g., Shadish *et al.* 2002). However, both of these areas are important in intervention research and should not be overlooked. Indeed, it is hard to imagine mounting a program of intervention research without knowledge of each. In addition, developing a program theory that specifies malleable mediators, composing program materials that fit the organizational and cultural context, and anticipating factors that may affect the uptake of an intervention by practitioners are crucial if scientific knowledge is to affect practice.

Intervention research is a generative and creative process that involves the design, development, and dissemination of systematic change strategies. An important aspect of intervention research is that it incorporates activities that are intended to promote the implementation of programs by practitioners and the agencies in which they work. These activities are what distinguish effective interventions that are likely to be adopted into practice from those interventions that, even though effective, are unlikely to penetrate practice. Although effective interventions often have compelling characteristics (e.g., target processes that are causally related to social and health problems, have supporting data from well-controlled studies), interventions that penetrate practice have five additional features. These focus on factors that accelerate the uptake of an EBT by agencies and practitioners. They include ease of use; a clear specification of core content required to produce expected outcomes; fit with the policy and organizational context; guidelines for implementation and cultural adaptation; and outcomes that are readily observed by stakeholders. This integration of design, development, and dissemination distinguishes this book and, more generally, intervention research.

In this sense, intervention research is more than program evaluation. Arguably, program evaluators of the past could work without substantive expertise because they had advanced knowledge of research design and statistics. They were evaluation experts but not necessarily program or substantive experts. Intervention research is different. The researcher is not an outside methodological expert who evaluates a promising program. In intervention research, researchers and practitioners, sometimes joined by administrators, collaborate to design and develop programs. Intervention researchers must have expertise with both the problem and the program area. Because they participate in the design of programs, intervention researchers usually understand and contribute to theories of change that underpin programs. The researcher's involvement in the development of the causal logic of a program permits better specification of both proximal and distal outcomes. Equally important, a theory of change guides mediation analyses by identifying the active ingredients of programs.

The design and development activities we describe do not initially require substantial funding. Although funding is usually required for efficacy and effectiveness trials, researchers and program developers can undertake much of the work described in the first four chapters without substantial financial support. Funding should not be a barrier to either the specification of a program theory or the development of a program manual. Moreover, once these essential components have been developed, it becomes easier to secure funding for testing and refining program components.

Perhaps more than other kinds of research (e.g., survey research), intervention research is essential for professions because professions must develop a knowledge base for practice. A foundational element of this knowledge base involves the design and development of practice strategies—that we have interchangeably called interventions and programs. In developing these practice strategies, this book describes five steps:

1. Specify a problem and develop program theory
2. Create and revise program materials
3. Refine and confirm program components
4. Assess the effectiveness of programs in a variety of settings and circumstances
5. Disseminate findings and program materials

This approach extends the perspective of Rothman and Thomas (1994) by placing more emphasis on program theory and the development of treatment manuals. In developing program materials, we describe a series of activities integrated across all five steps in intervention research. These activities involve the formulation, revision, differentiation, and translation/adaptation of manuals and other materials, such as implementation guides (see Figure 4.1). In Steps 1 and 2, manuals and other materials are born from the specification of a program theory that identifies malleable mediators which provide focal points for intervention (see, e.g., DePanfilis and Dubowitz 2005). In Steps 3 and 4, a sequential process of refining and confirming programs in quasi-experimental and experimental studies is described. Finally, we discuss in Step 5 the issues of dissemination, adaptation, and diffusion.

Methodological Issues in Intervention Research

Although the core theory supporting experimental and quasi-experimental design in the social sciences was developed more than 75 years ago (e.g., Fisher 1935), intervention research continues today to be a developing field. It requires broad knowledge of social or health problems and practice contexts. In addition, it requires skill in working with practitioners, administrators, consumers, citizen groups, data analysts, other researchers, and policy makers. Beyond these demands on researchers per se, at least four methodological challenges confront the field of intervention research. These are:

- ongoing tension between adaptation and fidelity,
- the clustering of human behavior and group randomized designs,
- selection bias when random assignment fails or is not possible, and
- the assessment of the effects of programs that are continuously adapted to need and preference during the course of intervention.

Each of these challenges raises complexities that are on the cutting edge of methodological innovation. Each is briefly discussed below.

Tension between Adaptation and Fidelity: When Intervention Research Starts Anew

Given the expense of efficacy and effectiveness trials, it is not possible to test interventions in all contexts and with all possible populations. However, when an intervention has proven to be effective, inevitably it will be used with new populations in new settings. As discussed in Chapters 4 and 6, we argue for a collaborative and consensual process of adaptation to extrapolate programs for use with a new population or in a new setting. This collaborative process involves program and problem experts who, with agency-level support, review program theory for relevance and modify program materials. Collaborative adaptation is significantly different from *local adaptation* in which an individual practitioner makes decisions about deleting or altering program content to provide better fit to a particular case or to agency practice constraints. As convenient as local adaptation may appear, recent studies suggest that it has high potential to compromise the effectiveness of an evidence-based treatment (Elliott and Mihalic 2004).

We want to emphasize this dynamic tension between adaptation and fidelity. EBP relies on practice experience and client preference, as well as the best available evidence, in making intervention decisions. This implies that practitioners have a responsibility under EBP to temper programs based on their experience, the preferences of clients, and other practice contingencies. In social and behavioral interventions, this person-centered approach makes sense. However, to preserve the effectiveness of evidence-based treatments, program theory and implementation benchmarks must be clear. An evidence-based program delivered without fidelity cannot be expected to have reliable impact. At the same time, when an evidence-based program is delivered without adaptation to a new population, program participants may experience some content as irrelevant, inappropriate, or perhaps even culturally objectionable.

How can programs be adapted and yet delivered with fidelity? It is not easy. In our view, two kinds of adaptations may be warranted under EBP: (1) systems adaptation in order to improve fit with the service system, and (2) cultural adaptation in order to improve fit with the population. Systems adaptation should occur at the agency or organizational level when a program is screened for adoption. Cultural adaptation should be guided by a specification of core content constituting implementation benchmarks. Based on research, cultural adaptation involves tailoring theories of change and logic models to address culturally unique risk and protective processes that operate within the communities served by an agency. The design and development process starts anew when adaptation is so significant as to alter core content. In this sense, the creative spark that ignites intervention research reaches its flashpoint because of friction between fidelity and adaptation.

Design of Randomized Experiments in Practice

A key aspect of intervention research is developing and testing interventions by using scientific methods, especially randomized controlled trials. Once maligned as unethical (because treatment may be withheld from the control group), random assignment is now accepted as the method of choice for determining the effectiveness of social and health services interventions. This is due in no small measure to two developments. First, the use of routine services or treatment as usual (TAU) for the control condition has replaced no-treatment control conditions as the recommended, ethically acceptable design of choice. This means that all research participants receive at least usual services and, as EBP spreads, it will mean that all research participants receive at least an evidence-based treatment (Doss and Atkins 2006). Indeed, many institutes and centers at the National Institutes of Health now prefer control conditions that qualify as evidence based (Office of Science Policy 2005). Second, experimental design has been separated (ever so slightly) from quantitative methods in the sense that mixed methods and qualitative methods are used increasingly to describe processes and outcomes in experimental studies. The use of qualitative methods in intervention research is providing a much clearer understanding of change processes and, in small studies where power does not permit quantitative analyses, it provides helpful descriptions of mediating mechanisms.

Random assignment is a probabilistic procedure, and so it tends to work when sample sizes are large. It is the best-known method for creating equivalence between two or more groups on both observed and unobserved measures. However, its strength is compromised when sample sizes are small. The probability theory on which random assignment relies is based on large samples. After randomization, we can usually compare groups and get a sense as to whether random assignment has worked well. But sometimes groups appear similar on observed measures, such as sociodemographic characteristics, and they differ on important unobserved measures, such as a risk factor for which data were not collected. This is the worst case scenario because failed random assignment may not be detected.

Two Challenges in Designing Studies with Random Assignment

Two challenges loom large in designing studies with random assignment: (1) randomizing when people are clustered in groupings such as families, neighborhoods, or agencies; and (2) handling randomization when it fails. The first challenge is related to advances in understandings of human behavior and the social environment. We appreciate more than ever the influence of nesting (i.e., a system within a system, such as a family unit within a community) on behavior and psychological adjustment. Indeed, adaptation across the life course is often thought of as a function of interactions between biological and environmental systems that are organized hierarchically. In social and behavioral research, this clustering, also known as *nestedness,* is manifest in the similarity of children within the same families, students in the same classrooms, and—at a higher order of clustering—schools within the same school districts, or factories within the same corporation. At still a higher order of clustering, nestedness is recognized as the similarity of individuals within the same organizations or geographical boundaries, such as voters within states. Clustering gives rise to methodological issues in randomizing that are especially difficult in pilot testing and efficacy trials. We discuss these issues below.

The second design challenge – failed randomization – is related to the issue of clustering. When a small number of units, such as schools or neighborhoods, is randomized to experimental and control conditions, random assignment is more likely to fail because the sample size is too small for probability mechanisms to work. When randomization fails, researchers have often used statistical methods like covariance analysis to control for group differences. In addition, sometimes researchers have tried to match participants in intervention groups with comparable participants from control groups. However, both of these approaches have serious limitations. Fortunately, new statistical procedures are being developed to help intervention researchers recover from failed randomization. These procedures may also be useful when randomization is not possible or when intervention and control groups are known to differ. We discuss this family of new procedures later on in the chapter.

Place-Based and Cluster Randomization

A core idea in the social and behavioral sciences is that people fill space in systematic ways. That is, social and psychological forces operate such that schools, neighborhoods, and communities can be distinguished based on demographic factors and, often, attitudes, beliefs, and behaviors. States are thought to have political dispositions ("red" versus "blue" states), and communities can be distinguished not only by their physical appearances but also by the kinds of social and health problems that predominate within their boundaries.

Although interventions are often targeted at the individual level, they may also be designed to affect a whole school's culture, the collective efficacy of a neighborhood, or the crime rate of a community. When the desired impact of an intervention is at the group or cluster level, it is appropriate to randomize at that level. Indeed, interventions are often designed to have a population-level impact. We hope to change local norms, to improve the public health, or to reduce population-level problems like the achievement gap or health disparities.

Methodologically, it is also appropriate to randomize at the group level when there is a threat of *treatment contamination*. By contamination, we mean that a study can be compromised when persons in a control group become aware of the intervention. This kind of contamination can happen by virtue of study participants' close association with others in the same cluster. Unplanned treatment dissemination in a control group can result in compensatory rivalry (i.e., attempts by control group members to replicate intervention outcomes without the benefit of the intervention); demoralization (i.e., disappointment at missing the opportunity to participate in the intervention); and other confounds that result from group assignment but not from the intervention per se.

Group level studies are likely to become more important in the future, and they already loom large in school- and community-based research. In the last 10 years, group and cluster randomized designs have been used to evaluate public health interventions. In the text box, read about the Progresa study of the impact of an education, health, and nutrition program on rates of growth and anemia in infants and young children in Mexico (Rivera, Sotres-Álvarez, Habicht, Shamah, and Billapando 2004).

Group-randomized trials, such as Progresa, implement promising intervention strategies on a large scale. The Progresa study randomized communities in order to observe a community effect. However, there is also a technical reason for randomizing at the group level when people are clustered, whether in terms of communities, neighborhoods, schools, work sites, or other aggregations. Because people within clusters tend to be similar, these similarities will suppress the variation observed for tests of significance. The variation will be too small and as a result, tests of significance are likely to overestimate the significance of differences between experimental and control groups. Whenever clustering is present,

---

Progresa:
The Impact of an Education, Health, and Nutrition Program in Mexico

---

About half of the 11 million deaths per year of children less than five years of age across the globe are due to malnourishment. Malnourishment is especially invidious in lesser developed countries where some 25% of children have too little to eat (Black, Morris, and Bryce 2003). Dr. Juan Rivera and his colleagues decided to do something about this. With the support of the Mexican government, they evaluated a community-level incentive-based welfare program for rural low-income families. The goal of Progresa was to provide food supplements to underweight children and to improve human capital by providing two kinds of cash transfers. The first cash transfer was universal, and this assistance was available to anyone participating in a food supplement program and Progresa-sponsored baby clinics where health education was provided along with routine health checkups and immunizations. The second cash transfer was contingent on the school attendance of school-age children in participating families. In total, cash transfers amounted to 20–30% percent of household income; less than 1% of families were denied payment for failure to comply. The study was conducted in six states in the central region of Mexico, where 506 communities were randomized to receive the intervention immediately or to a crossover condition, which received the intervention one year later.

At the end of one year, children in intervention communities had significantly higher hemoglobin levels and significantly lower rates of anemia (44.3% versus 54.9%) when compared to children in control group communities. In addition, moderation analyses revealed a significant effect for the youngest children in the poorest communities. Children less than six months of age who lived in the very poorest communities were significantly taller than children from the poorest communities in the crossover control group. Though still below the World Health Organization's standards, growth benefits were observed in the children who had the greatest potential for response to the intervention, that is, the most vulnerable children. Progresa is one of the first well-controlled, community-based studies to show a positive effect of education, nutritional supplements, and cash transfers on health. A group-randomized trial, Progresa is now being replicated around the world.

the researcher must consider group randomization and methods of analysis that properly estimate group differences.

Guidelines for Group Randomization

The literature on trials using group randomization is complicated, and presents statistical, design, and practical challenges that are beyond the scope of this book. However, based on our experience and extending Cook (2005), we offer three rules for designing studies when participants are nested or clustered.

Rule 1: Estimate the size of the intraclass correlation (ICC) and develop program theory to explain the ICC

The ICC is a measure of the percent of total variation that can be explained by clustering. When the ICC is zero, the effect of clustering is zero and statistical tests will not be biased. However, when the ICC is not zero, clustering will affect statistical significance and the power to determine significance. It is always a good idea to understand why clustering might be present in the study sample. For example, in testing *Making Choices,* we often observed a nontrivial ICC because children in a classroom had the same teacher and they were exposed to the same physical school environment. In addition, their friendship networks tended to be comprised largely of classmates. Therefore, teacher, classroom, and peer influences caused children within classrooms to share many experiences that influenced their attitudes, beliefs, and behaviors. Students in the same classroom could not be considered independent, and thus our research designs and data analyses needed to account for classroom clustering.

Rule 2: Randomize at the lowest level indicated by program theory and the ICC

From a statistical power perspective, it is usually desirable to randomize at the individual level; however, when ICCs are not trivial, you may not be able to randomize individuals. In the case of an elementary school study there are several levels of nesting: students are nested in classrooms, classrooms in schools, schools in districts, and districts in states. At each level, we can expect an ICC that is not zero. At what level should randomization take place?

Program theory is the guide. If implementation is at the classroom level, it is usually best to randomize at that level. That is, *randomize at the level of intervention implementation*, and then measure outcomes at all levels. Indeed, we recommend measuring not only outcomes at all levels but also measuring communication within and across levels. Although it may not be necessary to quantify cross- and within-level communication, it is often quite helpful to have an understanding of these levels of communication. For example, interviews with teachers may help in developing an understanding of the extent to which children from different classrooms, from different grades, and from different schools have opportunities to interact. Self-report data from children on their friendship networks could be useful in determining cross- and within-classroom communication. Whenever participants are nested in multiple layers of influence, the ICC will be based largely on communication patterns. Randomization should occur at the intervention level, and communication should be documented with sufficient detail to describe potential sources of within and across cluster variation.

Rule 3: Consider higher level covariates

Sometimes, the ICC can be reduced by including higher order covariates. The statistical models used to assess program outcomes are quite flexible. The models can include individual level covariates such as ethnicity, gender, or age. In addition, the models can include cluster-level covariates, such as school size, the leadership style of the principal, and per-pupil expenditures. In a study with a classroom-level intervention, teacher education (master's degree or not) and years of teaching might be entered as classroom-level covariates. These covariates could explain some of the between-classroom variation and reduce the ICC. However, if the number of higher order units is small, cluster-level covariates can be costly because each reduces degrees of freedom and, therefore, reduces the statistical power.

As we mentioned earlier, failure to adjust estimates of treatment effects for clustering can bias study findings. Indeed, this failure renders questionable the findings of many prior studies in social work and other professions. For example, in research on case management, cases within the caseloads of the same workers are not independent; they are nested within the worker. Clustering of cases within workers affects outcomes. If it is not controlled, the effect of case management is likely to be over-estimated. Similarly, outcomes in family therapy related to child adjustment may be nested in families and, depending on agency practices, families may be nested within therapist caseloads. If the researcher does not adjust estimates to account for family and therapist nesting, any comparisons of child outcomes are likely to be wrong. In the same way that Progresa adjusted findings for the clustering of children within communities, most intervention studies must consider nesting of participants in systems of influence.

Clustering raises practical challenges in conducting pilot tests and small efficacy studies where the power to detect a treatment effect must always be considered. If randomization has to take place at the agency level (e.g., nursing homes, schools, hospitals), a small efficacy trial may need 20 or more agencies to have adequate power to detect a treatment effect. Such a study becomes very involved. To test a family intervention in an efficacy trial, it may be necessary to have 20–30 clinicians participating in the trial to estimate a treatment effect conditioned on the nesting of families within caseloads. One potential strategy in these situations involves sampling fewer units within clusters and drawing more clusters for randomization. In the case of a school study, for example, we might sample fewer students within schools but include more schools in the sample. On balance, it is the number of clusters and not the number of participants within clusters that affects statistical power.

Selection Bias When Randomization Fails or Cannot
Be Used: Propensity Scores

When randomization fails or is impossible, post intervention differences between experimental and control (or comparison) groups may be confounded with pretreatment group differences. As we discussed in Chapter 5, this is called *selection bias*. The term *bias* is used to imply broadly that the effect of an intervention may not be due to the program but instead is the result of differences between participants in the treatment condition and those in the control condition. The putative effect is biased. This difference occurs, for example, when participants are allowed to volunteer for an intervention and then compared to participants who do not volunteer, or when participants are assigned to a condition because of high need and then compared to lower-need participants. In the first case, we might expect people who volunteer for an intervention—technically those who are *self-selected*—to be more motivated to comply with study requirements than those who did not volunteer. This type of higher motivation could affect outcomes. In the second case, we might expect people who are assigned to an intervention because of need—sometimes called *administratively* or *bureaucratically selected*—to differ from those in the comparison group. The lower need of people in the comparison condition could account for differences in outcomes.

Selection bias threatens quasi-experiments where random assignment is not used and experiments where random assignment is used but the sample size is simply too small for it to produce balanced groups. In cluster-randomized designs where large entities, such as schools, are being assigned, between-group balance can be compromised by having too few schools (or whatever the unit of randomization). Other times random assignment may be used, but post-randomization processes (e.g., differential attrition, compensatory rivalry) corrupt the equivalence of groups. Whether due to selection bias in quasi-experiments, failed randomization in experiments, or processes operating after group assignment, systematic differences between experimental and control or comparison groups create serious problems in estimating program effects.

Covariance Analysis to Control for Selection Bias

Historically, when researchers suspected that randomization failed or when it was impossible to use, they tested for between-group differences and, when found, they controlled for them statistically. As used here, the term *control* implies a statistical modeling process that removes the contribution of confounding variables to the outcome prior to the estimation of a program impact. Often called *covariance analysis*, this statistical method has been accepted for many years as a preferred method of dealing with selection and other biasing effects. Consider a routine regression equation for the outcome, Y_i:

$$Y_i = \alpha + \tau W_i + \beta X_i + e_i,$$

where W_i is a dichotomous variable indicating intervention, and X_i is the vector of independent variables for case i.

In this approach, we wish to estimate the effect (τ) of treatment (W) on Y_i by controlling for observed confounding variables (X_i). Hundreds of studies have used this approach.

Recently, however, scholars have raised questions about the assumptions that underpin the use of statistical controls when random assignment is compromised. When randomization is compromised, the correlation between W and e may not be equal to zero. As a result, the ordinary least square estimator of the effect of intervention (τ) may be biased and inconsistent. This is because W is not exogenous when random assignment is compromised. In fact, W is determined by a variety of other factors that may be either observed or unobserved. In addition, W is sometimes correlated with Y in the presence of selection effects (i.e., selection bias). The efficiency of statistical controls in *partialling out* selection effects will depend on whether selection is adequately measured by observed covariates, X. If relevant variables are missing, estimates of the intervention effect will be biased. All of this suggests that the use of covariance analysis is conditioned on assumptions that are easily violated and, when assumptions are violated, the traditional regression approach may not be the best choice (Guo and Fraser in press).

Propensity Scores and Other Advances in Modeling Selection Bias

So what can you do when randomization fails or is impossible? The key strategy is to rebalance the experimental and control groups by using one of several new statistical procedures. A central feature of most of these approaches is that they try to model selection bias. In doing so, the idea is to represent a combination of factors as a single number called a *propensity score*. The propensity score distinguishes experimental from control group participants. That is, the structure of selection is estimated for all participants, whether they are in the experimental or the control condition, as a probability of (propensity for) being in the intervention condition. The propensity score can then be used to match or weight participants in the experimental and control groups. This whole process is based on the somewhat inscrutable idea that even people in the control condition have a probability—based on their characteristics—of being in the intervention condition. Recall that you already know that the experimental and control conditions differ systematically, that selection bias is a problem because of failed randomization or because groups were assigned in some nonrandom fashion such as self-selection or administrative assignment.

The propensity score is used to statistically balance groups. Early approaches simply used propensity scores to pair control to experimental group members in 1 : 1 matches. However, recent efforts have developed algorithms to multiply match treatment participants to several control group participants with similar propensity scores. Furthermore, new ways have been developed to weight different control group matches to optimize similarity with participants in experimental groups.

It is beyond the scope of this book to describe these rapidly developing methods. Suffice it to say, these developments in statistical analysis hold great promise, not just for when randomization fails, but also for when it is impossible to randomize because of ethical or other reasons. To be sure, statistical methods do not replace random assignment. It is not yet clear whether propensity score approaches produce the kind of balance that can be achieved with large samples and proper random assignment. Propensity score approaches have the potential only to balance groups on observed measures. The advantage of random assignment is that, when it is implemented with large enough samples, it balances groups on both observed and unobserved measures. Nonetheless, the class of new statistical procedures that makes use of propensity and similar scores offers a range of new methods for analyzing data from experimental and quasi-experimental designs, including the estimation of treatment effects for different levels of treatment exposure (i.e., efficacy subset analyses based on dosage). To explore these new procedures, see Guo and Fraser (in press).

Dynamical Systems Modeling of Adaptive Interventions: Beyond the Randomized Controlled Trial

Throughout much of the history of intervention research, interventions have been conceptualized as invariant or *fixed* (Collins, Murphy, and Bierman 2004). That is, research participants assigned to an intervention condition have received what is considered to be the same treatment. In the standard randomized controlled trial (RCT; recall the example of the drug trial in Chapter 5), the intervention is provided in one common dosage that is not allowed to vary. In part, research design is based on this binary conceptualization: people either receive the intervention or they do not. However, this either-or scenario does not reflect the gradations in which much of practice operates. In practice, dosage is often determined by need. People with greater need receive more intervention. Dosage varies across people, but it can also vary within people. For example, a person's needs may change over time and so the level of service may vary based on changing needs. Therefore, fixing an intervention at a standard dosage is inconsistent with good practice.

One of the great challenges in intervention research is the development of research methods to evaluate practice as it really happens. In adaptive interventions, the composition of an intervention and its dosage are not fixed. Many interventions have this feature. In the Casey Family Program (see Chapter 1), services were assigned after comprehensive and recurring case assessments. Over the course of a child's stay in enhanced foster care, the type and amount of service varied based on these need assessments. In juvenile justice, the surveillance associated with probation is increased when youths are thought to be at a higher risk of reoffending. In mental health, case managers periodically adjust the mix of supportive services that are "wrapped around" an adult with a serious mental illness. In practice, the number, nature, and amount (i.e., dosage) of services are often adapted based on client need and preference.

This pattern of providing services based on need occasionally leads to a very curious evaluation finding: Greater provision of services is associated with poorer service outcomes. Because greater need is usually associated with greater adversity and dysfunction, this greater adversity and dysfunction are often—but not always—associated with higher service involvement and a higher probability of poor service outcomes. Because need is usually a function of complicated comorbidities and environmental crises or stresses, adaptive interventions must be evaluated in the context of differential need and the latent decision-making rules that practitioners use to allocate intervention resources.

Accounting for the continuous adaptation of services to meet the changing needs and preferences of clients is one of the emerging challenges in intervention research. Work in this area is giving rise to new ways of thinking about interventions and innovative methods for assessing outcomes. These innovations involve the application of highly flexible modeling techniques, such as generalized additive mixture models (Brown *et al.* 2008), which permit monitoring the trajectories of subgroups of program participants as they experience an intervention over time. Some of these innovations involve also dynamical or simulation algorithms. In the next section, we apply one of these approaches to the Elementary School Success Profile (ESSP), which is the elementary school version of the SSP.

The Elementary School Success Profile as an
Adaptive Intervention

The ESSP is an adaptive intervention that attempts to guide decisional processes in formulating school-based interventions for children (for a full description of the ESSP, see Bowen 2008). After completing the ESSP assessment, students are referred for services that are matched to their risk profiles. Based on available resources, the composition of these services is individualized to the student's needs as determined by a student's scores in various risk and protective factor domains on the ESSP. Scores within these domains influence both the composition of services and recommended dosages. The ESSP may be readministered at several assessment points, and a student's scores can be used to reconfigure services.

From a dynamical systems modeling perspective, we can think of the profile score as a *tailoring variable,* a measure used to determine the nature and amount of services (Collins *et al.* 2004). That is, the ESSP can be conceptualized as an adaptive intervention comprised of three components: evidence-based tailoring variables (i.e., a profile of the social and academic performance of children in schools); decision rules (i.e., threshold points on risk scores indicating referral for different kinds of services); and implementation guidelines for the use of the ESSP. Note that from this perspective the actual services to which students are referred are not considered part of the ESSP intervention. They are determined by school resources and decisions made in consultation with parents, school staff, and others.

The success of the ESSP as an adaptive intervention is related to: (1) the validity of the tailoring variables (i.e., school success profiles) in distinguishing children with high needs from those with low needs; (2) the capacity of the instrument to measure the tailoring variables accurately (especially reliable assessment over time); (3) the precision of the decision rules for recommending referral based on students' scores; and (4) the extent to which school officials have resources and follow through to ensure that referral results in actual service involvement. Although the ESSP formalizes the assessment of tailoring variables and specifies decision criteria more explicitly than is common in current practice, the ESSP might be considered a somewhat typical adaptive intervention because it results in differential service provision based on need profiles.

Adaptive interventions can be evaluated in the same way as fixed interventions. That is, random assignment to experimental and control groups is preferred, and the effect of an intervention is assessed as a group difference between experimental and control conditions. However, because the dose is systematically manipulated based on the tailoring variables and decision rules, the dose cannot be used as a moderator (Recall that because dose introduces selection effects in efficacy subsets, it is difficult to use in studies of fixed interventions as well). Indeed, assuming

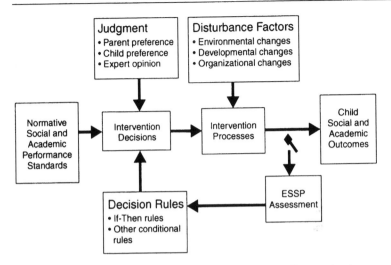

Figure 7.1. Dynamical model of elementary school success profile: an adaptive intervention.

that the intervention was implemented as intended, we already know that systematic differences exist between participants in low versus high dose categories. If we wish to find out whether decision processes worked to provide more services to those participants with greater need and whether this produced a desirable result, data must be modeled as a *dynamical system*. A dynamical system is a multivariate, time-varying process in which changes in outcomes are viewed as a function of changes in inputs or, in the case of adaptive interventions, of changes in tailoring variables (Rivera, Pew, and Collins 2007).

For the ESSP, a dynamical model can be portrayed as a simple diagram (see Figure 7.1). At the child level, the goal of the ESSP is to improve social and academic outcomes in schools. This goal is shown on the right of Figure 7.1 as a function of Intervention Processes that are determined by an Intervention Decision, which is used in the ESSP to adapt service recommendations to the unique profile of each child. Intervention Decisions are influenced by local normative values for Social and Academic Performance and by Judgment, which represents both the collective input of students, parents, teachers, and other experts (e.g., a speech and language therapist) and their preferences regarding interventions (e.g., after-school tutoring). In this sense, the ESSP is consistent with the EBP principles because it incorporates a mechanism for collaborative decision making regarding the composition and dosage of intervention services.

However, the key feature of the ESSP is the dynamical nature of assessment and the decision-making process. The ESSP incorporates a *disturbance term*, which represents the changing needs of a child as a function of a range of environmental, developmental, and organizational influences. The fit of intervention processes to a child's constellation of needs is seen as a function of *disturbance factors*, which represent changes in child development and a host of other factors inside and outside the school (e.g., staff competencies and preferences, school resources, funding). These include both risk and protective factors. For example, a child's living situation could improve significantly because of changes in parental employment. This change would constitute a protective effect that might alter the need for an intervention. Alternatively, the loss of a parent or parental unemployment could elevate risk for social or academic problems and change a child's level of need for or responsiveness to interventions.

The ESSP Assessment box in Figure 7.1 is shown as a switch that periodically "turns on" and triggers a new assessment that redefines decision inputs via if-then and other conditional statements. That is, periodic reassessment by the ESSP provides new input on the tailoring variables—the child's school success profile—and, if a child reaches a threshold point established by the ESSP, a parent-child-teacher conference is initiated to revise intervention strategies based on the school's available resources and involving the judgment of others who may be involved in the child's life.

This type of dynamical systems modeling lies at the heart of intervention research when interventions are adapted based on changing needs or risk status. We have used an individual-level example, but the collective profiles of students on tailoring variables can be used as a basis for collective interventions. For example, the ESSP may be used to identify the aggregate needs of students in a classroom or a school. It can function, then, as a basis not only for the design of individual adaptive interventions, but also for universal preventive interventions that are adapted to the needs of students clustered in classrooms, schools, or other aggregations.

The challenge in dynamical systems modeling is to improve client outcomes by optimizing the flow of information and the precision of decision rules. To date, the ESSP has been administered only two or three times during the school year. That level of reassessment is not frequent enough for the continuous feedback on which many adaptive interventions depend. However, a strength of the ESSP is the rigor of its decisional processes. Unlike case management and other adaptive interventions where workers make incremental clinical judgments (and, if they subscribe to EBP, involve clients in intervention decisions), the ESSP provides for a systematic review. The tailoring variables in the ESSP are based on research, so there is an empirical foundation for decision rules. In full operation, decision rules would be constantly fine-tuned based on continually collected data at each point in the ESSP process.

Quite different from the experimental and control group designs that characterize much intervention research today, dynamical systems modeling draws on process control principles from engineering. It has potential not just from the perspective of fitting observed data to a conceptual model (which is the way we analyze data in most research projects today) but also from the perspective of optimization through simulation. Frequently used in engineering and physics, optimization through simulation is rarely applied in the social and behavioral sciences. We discuss adaptive interventions for two reasons. First, because they represent routine practice in many venues; second, because the challenge of developing research methods to test adaptive interventions presents new possibilities beyond the RCT. Dynamical modeling of intervention processes could be the basis for significant advances in better fitting intervention research methods to the way practice really happens (for a detailed explanation with another example, see Rivera *et al.* 2007).

Ethics: The Independence of the Intervention Researcher

Finally, the very involvement of researchers in the design and development of the interventions they evaluate creates special concern regarding the independence of the investigator. Discussed throughout the book, intervention research is a synthesis of program development and program evaluation. In this sense, it is an amalgamation of two important fields. The integration of program development with program evaluation requires that the researcher become involved intimately in program design. However, this involvement violates the highly valued view that evaluators should be impartial and independent of program providers. In the traditions of logical positivism, the independence of the researcher is thought to provide an objectivity that is critical for rigorous and critical program assessment.

But, as we have emphasized, the researcher is deeply involved in the intervention research process, especially in specifying a program theory and developing program materials. This involvement leads to an investment in the specification of outcome measures, in the delivery of a program with fidelity, and in careful consideration of the practice context in which programs may ultimately be adopted. Often considered strengths of intervention research, these should produce better measurement and more carefully specified programs.

Notwithstanding these strengths, the researcher's involvement also creates vested interest in observing positive evaluation outcomes and, if a program is disseminated, this involvement may represent the potential for reaping financial benefit from sales of treatment manuals, contracts to provide training, and honoraria for speaking engagements. Thus, the lack of independence between the researcher and the researched program yields potential conflicts of interest. In this context, professional codes of conduct become especially important. Researchers are expected to collect and analyze data using scientific methods and to approach the process of evaluation with integrity. Both scientific rigor and intellectual honesty are expected. The principle of independence must be considered, and after data support initial efficacy and effectiveness, programs found to be effective should be independently evaluated.

Conclusion

We started this book with the idea of "making a difference." In truth, you can make a difference without doing intervention research. You can organize a community to fight crime, lead a strategic reform in your agency, provide food supplements to families in the poorest neighborhoods, or befriend and advocate for a lonely maltreated child. Not everything needs to be evaluated. Indeed, intervention research begins when you begin to feel that a particular pattern of "making a difference" works consistently in practice.

We need to develop and test these patterns of making a difference because they hold the potential to help many others. New and promising interventions should be subjected to rigorous testing so, if effective, they can be used with other persons or communities in similar local or national circumstances. We also need to broaden our perspective and assume a more global stance. The massive social and health problems across the globe often have social origins. In the words of Dr. Michael Marmot, chair of the Commission on Social Determinants of Health at the World Health Organization:

> The gross inequalities . . . that we see within and between countries present a challenge to the world. That there should be a spread of life expectancy of 48 years among countries and 20 years or more within countries is not inevitable. A burgeoning volume of research identifies social factors at the root of much of these inequalities. (2005, 1099)

The factors that cause social and health problems, such as social and environmental conditions that result from ill-advised public policies— and those that result in life expectancy and other health disparities—are malleable. They can be changed. Historically, we have had neither the will nor the technology to address these factors. But that situation is changing. Interventions like Progresa represent a growing commitment across the globe to developing the technology, the programs, and the policies to alter the social and environmental conditions that compromise so much human potential.

In this book, we have outlined a five-step process for developing and evaluating programs that might contribute to this effort. We illustrated how to craft a program theory and how from that to design an intervention. We described a strategy for developing treatment manuals, and we discussed a rigorous process of testing programs. Finally, we specified the challenges of disseminating programs and, in this chapter, of continuing to develop intervention research methods.

Intervention research is not for the faint of heart. It is creative and innovative. It can also be tedious and frustrating. It is a research method that requires a deep understanding of practice. What's more intervention research is theoretical and requires mastery of the literature. It is analytical, involving skill in data and text analysis and in the linkage of research findings to practice concepts and behavior. Intervention research is also political because it focuses on changing the status quo and often on social justice. It is foundational, because professions cannot exist without practice knowledge. In the end though, intervention research is rewarding. We hope you will join us in designing and developing interventions.

Additional Reading

Cook, Thomas D. (2005, May). Emergent principles for the design, implementation, and analysis of cluster-based experiments in social science. *The Annals of the American Academy of Political and Social Science, 599*: 176–198.

Guo, Shenyang, and Mark W. Fraser. (In press). *Propensity score matching: Statistical methods and applications.* Thousand Oaks, CA: Sage.

Rivera, Daniel E., Michael D. Pew, and Linda M. Collins. (2007). Using engineering control principles to inform the design of adaptive interventions: A conceptual introduction. *Drug and Alcohol Dependence, 88S*: S31–S40.

Glossary

Adaptation Modifications made to an intervention in order to tailor it to a new population or setting, taking into account research and practice knowledge.

Black Box Research Research that evaluates program outcomes without utilizing program theory; that is, without focusing on mechanisms that might explain causal relations between, for example, program processes and outcomes.

Cause a variable that produces an effect; what produces a result, e.g., specific intervention that results in a change in behavior.

Causal Inference In intervention research, the supposition that an observed outcome is the result of the experimental manipulation of a specific variable, usually the treatment condition. Causal inference requires that the cause precedes the effect, the cause covaries with the effect, and alternative explanations for the putative effect are ruled out.

Causal Model a diagram, often statistical in nature, that portrays the relationships among variables, often including mediators.

Change Score A score calculated from one administration of a survey to another administration of the same survey in order to estimate gain or loss, usually pretest to posttest difference score.

Comparison condition a group that is compared to the intervention group and receives routine services, an alternative intervention, or no intervention.

Coefficient a measure of the strength of a relationship between two variables or combinations of variables.

Cohort A group of people who share a similar characteristic, such as age, geographic location, or school grade.

Comparison Group *see* comparison condition.

Confounding Variable An extraneous variable that covaries with a variable of interest and interferes with interpretation of the study results.

Construct A concept that may not be directly observable (e.g., delinquency); researchers must develop measures for constructs.

Control Group A group that is assigned, often by random means, to no-treatment, to delayed treatment, or to an alternative treatment and serves as a comparison to an experimental group which receives a planned intervention.

Covariance Analysis A statistical modeling process that removes the contribution of confounding variables from estimates of program impacts. *Also called statistical control.*

Curriculum An intervention manual in which practice activities may, in part, be educational in nature and involve didactic processes.

Cutoff Score A specified score on an assessment instrument that indicates in regression-discontinuity designs assignment to either the intervention group or control group. For example, all participants who fall at or above the cutoff score will receive the treatment, whereas those that fall below the cutoff score will serve as the control group.

Decision Rules In an adaptive intervention, guidelines for the provision of intervention services; usually related to scores or threshold points on an assessment device (e.g., a risk assessment inventory).

Differentiation When developing an intervention manual, the process of adapting program content for alternative populations in the intended setting.

Diffusion The integration of evidence-based interventions into routine practice.

Distal Outcomes Outcomes observed in the longer term, such as school dropout, arrest, or child maltreatment.

Dose Amount of exposure to the intervention or treatment.

Dose Response Analysis A scientific method that estimates treatment effects for participants who receive the full dose of an intervention as compared to participants who receive less than the full dose. See Efficacy Subset Analysis.

Dynamical System A multivariate, time-varying process in which changes in outcomes are viewed as a function of changes in inputs, or in the case of adaptive interventions, of changes in tailoring variables.

Effect Size A standardized statistical estimate of the magnitude of a program's effect on desired outcomes. Examples include the standardized mean difference and correlation coefficient.

Effectiveness The strength of causal linkages between program processes and outcomes when an intervention is implemented under routine practice conditions.

Effectiveness Trial Research study designed to test whether an intervention produces a desired outcome when implemented under routine practice conditions. *Also called* effectiveness test.

Efficacy The strength of causal linkages between program processes and outcomes when an intervention is implemented in a highly controlled setting.

Efficacy Subset Analysis An analytic method that compares the outcomes of different groups of participants assigned to an intervention condition to the participants in comparison or control conditions. Groups are variably defined and selected based on exposure to or participation in the intervention. *See* Dose Response Analysis.

Efficacy Trial Research study designed to test whether an intervention produces a desired outcome when implemented in highly controlled (ideal) settings where alternative explanations can be ruled out. *Also called* efficacy tests.

Evaluative Processes In intervention research, the processes involved in estimating the impact of the intervention program.

Evidence-Based Intervention An intervention that has been evaluated using scientific methods with cumulative findings from several evaluations demonstrating effectiveness.

Evidence-Based Practice The systematic process of utilizing evidence gathered from scientific studies of interventions and programs to guide clinical and practice decisions.

Evidence-Based Treatment Practices that have been subjected to repeated, rigorous scientific research and have demonstrated effectiveness.

Experimental Condition In a research study, a group that has been assigned to receive the intervention being tested, as opposed to the control or comparison groups that do not receive the tested intervention. The term is sometimes reserved to describe only groups that are assigned randomly to the intervention condition. *Also called the* Intervention Condition.

Experimental Design Research design that involves randomly assigning participants to one or more intervention groups and one or more control groups.

External Validity The extent to which study outcomes (i.e., causal inferences) can be generalized beyond the sample to other persons, settings, and measures.

Factorial Approach In an intervention study, the process of testing all potentially important program components in order to refine and optimize an intervention.

Failure Case Analysis The practice of studying both successful and unsuccessful events, participants, or programs in order to inform the design of an intervention.

Fidelity The extent to which an intervention is delivered as intended without deviation from the specified protocol.

Focus Group A type of data collection that involves convening a small panel of people with a particular perspective or area of knowledge and facilitating a discussion to identify important themes, experiences, and/or views of that panel.

Implementation The delivery of the intervention program being tested.

Implementation Drivers Components of intervention implementation designed to improve a program's fidelity, such as staff training, supervisor and administrative support, and recruitment of qualified practitioners. May also include organizational factors such as climate and culture that affect the fidelity of implementation.

Incidence The number of new cases of a given condition in a given population at a specified time and area indicating the risk of developing that condition.

Inputs As part of a logic model, the resources needed to implement an intervention, such as staff, training, facilities, and equipment costs.

Intent-to-Treat Analysis An analysis in which all participants assigned to an intervention condition in an experiment are analyzed, regardless of whether or not participants receive a full or partial dose; an analysis based on group assignment and not level of participation in or exposure to an intervention.

Internal Validity The validity of causal inferences about a relationship between two or more variables; in intervention research, the degree to which one can assume that an intervention produced observed outcomes.

Interrupted Time-Series Design A quasi-experimental research design that involves establishing a series of baseline measurements, introducing an intervention, and then observing the subsequent measurements to see if a change in slope or intercept occurs as a result of the intervention.

Intervention a purposeful change strategy, whether at the individual, family, group, organizational, community, societal or other level; a program or policy intended to produce a change; used interchangeably with the term *program* in this book.

Intervention Condition In a research study, a group that has been assigned to receive the intervention being tested, as opposed to the control or comparison groups that do not receive the intended intervention.

Intervention Manual A guide to practice that describes a problem, a program theory, practice objectives, and program content.

Intervention Model A conceptual design outlining the theory, the goals, the activities, and the expected outcomes of an intervention program.

Intraclass Correlation (ICC) A statistical estimate of the percent of total variation in an outcome measure that can be explained by differences between groups or classes that are clustered hierarchically within other groups or classes.

Local Adaptation Program changes undertaken by practitioners to improve fit with local practice conditions.

Logic Model A graphic representation of a program's inputs and program components leading to expected outputs, intermediate outcomes, and distal outcomes.

Malleable Mediators Mediators identified as being responsive to intervention and influential in affecting distal outcomes.

Measure An indicator of a variable of interest, e.g. grade point average and hours of study per week are measures or indicators of academic commitment.

Measurement Model A conceptualization of measures that often involves multiple constructs and indicators.

Mediator A variable that intervenes between a cause and an effect and is thought to transmit a causal influence; a variable that serves as a causal link, e.g., increases in skill may transmit the influence of participation in an intervention to proximal or distal outcomes.

Meta-Analysis A set of statistical techniques that combines results from multiple evaluations of the same or similar intervention in order to derive an overall estimate of the intervention's effect.

Methodological Pluralism The idea that knowledge development can be informed by using multiple research methods, that is, qualitative and quantitative methods.

Mixed-Methods Study A research study that utilizes both quantitative and qualitative methods.

Moderated Mediation When mediating mechanisms identified in an intervention's program theory operate differently for different populations or within different contexts (e.g., rural versus urban settings).

Moderator A variable, such as age, gender, or risk status (e.g., high versus low risk), that influences study results and indicates differential treatment effects for different populations.

Nestedness The clustering of a system of units within a system of units such as an individual within a family or a family within a community.

Outputs As part of an intervention logic model, the expected outcomes of an intervention usually identified as malleable mediators.

Partial Factorial Approach In an intervention study, the process of selecting promising program components and testing them in order to refine and optimize an intervention.

Path Chart A graphic representation of the active pathways in a risk chain.

Pilot Test A preliminary study, often using mixed methods, that tests intervention processes with the purpose of revising and refining a program before it goes to an efficacy trial.

Place-Based Intervention An intervention that focuses on the collective processes of a specific group of people who share common space and who often subscribe to common goals and values.

Post-Randomization Effects A threat to internal validity that occurs when particular events, such as attrition, affect randomized groups and compromise between-group equivalence, confounding the study results.

Post-test Data Follow-up data gathered after the implementation of an intervention is completed.

Practice Guidelines A set of general, decision-making tools based on research evidence and expert practitioner consensus that aid in the selection of interventions appropriate for a target population and a targeted outcome.

Practice Penetration The rate of participation among those approached to participate in an intervention; also the representativeness of participants in an intervention or program. *Also called* Reach.

Practice Protocol A set standardized procedural guidelines for a specific area of practice.

Prescriptive Intervention An intervention that is guided by specific principles and protocols that are described in a set of explicit guidelines or steps, such as a treatment manual.

Pretest Data Baseline data gathered before implementation of an intervention.

Prevalence The total number of cases of a given condition in a given population at a specified time and area.

Problem Theory Conceptual understanding derived from considering the individual and environmental conditions that give rise to a problem or sustain it over time.

Program Drift Program changes that occur after intervention implementation due to a variety of factors concerning program supervision, such as lowered commitment to the program, less intensive training of staff, and organizational conflicts that affect an intervention's fidelity.

Program Effect An outcome that results from the implementation of an intervention or program.

Program Elements or Program Factors Specific components that make up an intervention.

Program Integrity In intervention research, the degree to which an intervention is implemented as intended. *See* fidelity

Program Theory A conceptualization of the causal logic of an intervention by specifying and matching intervention methods to a range of proximal and distal outcomes and describing how intervention activities are expected to produce significant effects.

Propensity Score An estimation of the probability of each study participant to be assigned to the intervention group, based on the assumption that all participants have some likelihood for being randomly chosen for the intervention. The score is used to match participants in intervention and control groups in order to control for selection effects.

Protective factors An asset or strength that acts to buffer the negative effects of a risk factor and increases the likelihood of experiencing a positive outcome.

Proximal outcomes Outcomes observed in the short term, such as self-efficacy, coping skills, or changes in behavior. Often considered to mediate distal outcomes.

Quasi-Experimental Design Research design that involves non-random assignment of participants to one or more intervention groups and one or more comparison groups.

Random Assignment The process of assigning participants in a study to treatment or control groups on the basis of chance to ensure that each participant has a nonzero probability of being assigned to each condition.

Randomized Controlled Design (RCT) A research design in which participants are randomly assigned to an intervention group or a control group and their outcomes are compared to detect possible intervention effects.

Reach the extent to which a program or intervention gets to the intended population. See practice penetration.

Regression Discontinuity Design A quasi-experimental research design that involves assigning intervention and comparison groups on the basis of a cutoff score.

Reliability The likelihood that a program or a measure will produce consistent results repeatedly over time.

Replicability The extent to which a research study or program is reproducible by other researchers or practitioners.

Research Design The systematic process of structuring all elements of a research study, including the sampling and recruitment plan, the number of groups or conditions, the group assignment mechanism, the explanatory and outcome measures, the data collection strategy, and analytic methods.

Resilience A developmental perspective that describes the processes that enable a person to develop normative behaviors in the presence of adversity or risk.

Risk factors individual and environmental conditions that increase the likelihood for negative outcomes in a particular population.

Scale Conditions Providing a program under real-world practice conditions in which the researchers have limited ability to control implementation.

Sequential Experimentation The process of conducting a sequence of experimental and quasi-experimental studies to test competing program elements in order to optimize the development of an intervention.

Selection Bias Group differences that confound causal inference about the effect of an intervention and are usually the result of nonrandom assignment processes.

Semi-Structured Interview An interview conducted with a preset structure of guiding questions that focus on a particular theme and allow for a degree of flexibility in information gathered.

Statistical Power The probability of correctly rejecting the null hypothesis, or correctly finding a treatment effect when an effect exists. Among other factors, statistical power is related to the size of the sample, variation within the sample, level of statistical significance (e.g., $p<.05$), and the size of the treatment effect.

Survey A set of questions, usually multiple-choice, that is administered in a research study to gather information about participants, program providers, the program context, etc.

Tailoring Variable In an adaptive intervention, a measure used to determine the nature and amount of intervention a participant receives based on individual characteristics.

Theory of Change In intervention research, a graphic depiction of the causal chain of program activities intended to produce a positive intervention outcome.

Translational Research A branch of intervention research that focuses on the adoption, implementation, and diffusion of research-supported interventions in practice.

Treatment Contamination When participants assigned to a control condition learn about the content of an intervention condition.

Treatment Group In a research study, the group assigned to receive an intervention or treatment being tested.

Treatment Manual A written protocol for a specific intervention; a guide that outlines program theory or principles and gives detailed explanations of program content and activity.

Treatment-as-Usual Control Condition In a research study, a group that is assigned to receive routine services instead of a tested intervention and is used as a comparison to the experimental group. In social and behavior research, this condition is accepted as the standard control or comparison condition.

Validity The extent to which an assessment instrument measures what it is intended to measure; also the degree of support for an inference, its truth.

Waitlist Control Group Design A research study that involves assigning the comparison or control groups to a waitlist condition that receives the intervention on delay, sometimes called a crossover design

Waitlist Group In a research study, a group that receives the intervention on delay, serving as the control group during the study, and receiving the intervention after the study. Waitlist groups are used when it is undesirable or unethical to deny receipt of treatment.

References

Aarons, Gregory A. (2004). Mental health provider attitudes toward adoption of evidence-based practice: The evidence-based practice attitude scale (EBPAS). *Mental Health Services Research*, 6(2): 61–74.

Abrahamson, Daniel J. (1999). Outcomes, guidelines, and manuals: On leading horses to water. *Clinical Psychology: Science and Practice*, 6(4): 467–471.

Addis, Michael E. (1997). Evaluating the treatment manual as a means of disseminating empirically validated psychotherapies. *Clinical Psychology: Science and Practice*, 4(1): 1–11.

Addis, Michael E., and Aaron D. Krasnow. (2000). A national survey of practicing psychologists' attitudes toward psychotherapy treatment manuals. *Journal of Consulting and Clinical Psychology*, 68(2): 331–399.

Addis, Michael E., Wendy A. Wade, and Christina Hatgis. (1999). Barriers to evidence based practices: Addressing practitioners' concerns about manual based psychotherapies. *Clinical Psychology: Science and Practice*, 6(4): 430–441.

Allison, Mandy A., Lori A. Crane, Brenda L. Beaty, Arthur J. Davidson, Paul Melinkovich, and Allison Kempe. (2007). School-based health centers: Improving access and quality of care for low-income adolescents. *Pediatrics*, 120(4): 887–894.

American Psychiatric Association. (2000). *Diagnostic and statistical manual of mental disorders IV- TR*. Washington, DC: American Psychiatric Association.

Bacallao, Martica L., and Paul R. Smokowski. (2005). "Entre dos mundos" (between two worlds): Bicultural skills training with Latino immigrant families. *Journal of Primary Prevention, 26*(6): 485–509.

Barrera, Jr., Manual, and Filipe G. Castro. (2006). A heuristic framework for the cultural adaptation of interventions. *Clinical Psychology: Science and Practice, 13*(4): 311–316.

Beck, Aaron T., John A. Rush, Brian F. Shaw, and Gary Emery. (1979). *Cognitive therapy of depression.* New York: Guilford Press.

Berleman, William C., James R. Seaberg, and Thomas W. Steinburn. (1972). Delinquency prevention experiment of the Seattle Atlantic Street Corner: Final evaluation. *Social Service Review, 46*(3): 323–446.

Bickman, Leonard. (1999). Practice makes perfect and other myths about mental health services. *American Psychologist, 54*(11): 958–973.

Black, R. E., S. S. Morris, and J. Bryce. (2003). Where and why are 10 million children dying every year? *Lancet, 361*(9376): 2226–2234.

Blythe, Betty J., and Tony Tripodi. (1989). *Measurement in direct social work practice.* Beverly Hills, CA: Sage.

Bond, Gary R., Lisa Evans, Michelle P. Salyers, Jane Williams, and Hea-Won Kim. (2000). Measurement of fidelity in psychiatric rehabilitation. *Mental Health Services Research, 2*(2): 75–87.

Bowen, Gary L., Roderick Rose, and Natasha K. Bowen. (2005). *The reliability and validity of the School Success Profile.* Philadelphia: Xlibras.

Bowen, Gary L., Michael E. Woolley, Jack M. Richman, and Natasha K. Bowen. (2001). Brief intervention in schools: The School Success Profile. *Brief Intervention and Crisis Intervention, 1*(1): 43–54.

Bowen, Natasha K. (2006). Psychometric properties of the Elementary School Success Profile for children. *Social Work Research, 30*(1): 51–63.

Bowen, Natasha K. (2008). Cognitive testing and the validity of child-report data from the Elementary School Success Profile. *Social Work Research, 32*(1): 18–28.

Bowen, Natasha K., and Gary L. Bowen. (1999). Effects of crime and violence in neighborhoods and schools on the school behavior and performance of adolescents. *Journal of Adolescent Research, 14*(3): 319–342.

Bowen, Natasha K., Gary L. Bowen, and Michael E. Woolley. (2004). Constructing and validating assessment tools for school-based practitioners: The Elementary School Success Profile. In Albert R. Roberts, and Kenneth R. Yeager, (Eds.),*Evidence-based practice manual: Research and outcome measures in health and human services* (pp. 509–517). New York: Oxford University Press.

Brekke, John S., Kathleen Ell, and Lawrence Palinkas. (2007). Translational Science at the National Institute of Mental Health: Can Social Work Take Its Rightful Place? *Research on Social Work Practice, 17*(1): 123–133.

Briar, Scott. (1974). The future of social work. *Social Work 19*(5): 514–531.

Briar, Scott, and Henry Miller. (1971). *Problems and issues in social casework.* New York: Columbia University Press.

Brislin, Richard W. (1970). Back-translation for cross-cultural research. *Journal of Cross-Cultural Psychology, 1*(3): 185–216.

Bronfenbrenner, Urie.(1979). *The ecology of human development: Experiments by nature and design.* Cambridge, MA: Harvard University Press.

Brown, C. Hendricks, Wei Wang, Sheppard G. Kellam, Bengt O. Muthén, Hanno Petras, Peter Toyinbo, et al. (2008). Methods for testing theory and evaluating impact in randomized field trials: Intent-to-treat analyses for integrating the perspectives of person, place, and time. *Drug and Alcohol Dependence, 95S*: S74–S104.

Campbell, Donald T., and Julian C. Stanley (1963). *Experimental and quasi-experimental designs for research.* Chicago: Rand McNally.

Carroll, Kathleen M., and Kathryn F. Nuro. (2002). One size cannot fit all: A stage model for psychotherapy manual development. *Clinical Psychology: Science and Practice, 9*(4): 396–406.

Castro, Felipe G., Manual Barrera Jr., and Charles R. Martinez Jr. (2004). The cultural adaptation of prevention interventions: Resolving tensions between fidelity and fit. *Prevention Science, 5*(1): 41–45.

Centers for Disease Control and Prevention. (2007a). *Behavioral risk factor surveillance system.* http://www.cdc.gov/brfss/.

Centers for Disease Control and Prevention. (2007b). *Improving public health practice through translation research* (RFA–CD–07–005). Retrieved from http://grants.nih.gov/grants/guide/rfa-files/RFA-CD-07-005.html.

Centers for Disease Control and Prevention. (2007c). *Smoking and tobacco use.* http://www.cdc.gov/tobacco/data_statistics/tables/adult/table_2.htm.

Centers for Disease Control and Prevention. (2007d). *Youth risk behavior surveillance system.* http://www.cdc.gov/HealthyYouth/yrbs/index.htm.

Chambless, Dianne L., and Steven D. Hollon. (1998). Defining empirically supported therapies. *Journal of Consulting and Clinical Psychology, 66*(1): 7–18.

Chorpita, Bruce F. (2002). Treatment manuals for the real world: Where do we build them? *Clinical Psychology Science and Practice, 9*(4): 431–433.

Collins, Linda M., Susan A. Murphy, and Karen L. Bierman. (2004). A conceptual framework for adaptive preventive interventions. *Prevention Science, 5*(3): 185–196.

Collins, Linda M., Susan A. Murphy, and Victor J. Strecher. (2007). The multiphase optimization strategy (MOST) and the sequential multiple assignment randomized trial (SMART). *American Journal of Preventive Medicine, 32*(5S): S112–S118.

Cook, Thomas D. (2005). Emergent principles for the design, implementation, and analysis of cluster-based experiments in social science. *The Annals of the American Academy of Political and Social Science*, 599(1): 176–198.

Crick, Nicki R., and Kenneth A. Dodge. (1994). A review and reformulation of social information-processing mechanisms in children's social adjustment. *Psychological Bulletin*, 115(1): 74–101.

Crick, Nicki R., and Kenneth A. Dodge. (1996). Social information processing mechanisms in reactive and proactive aggression. *Child Development*, 67(3): 993–1002.

DePanfilis, Diane, and Howard Dubowitz. (2005). Family Connections: A program for preventing child neglect. *Child Maltreatment*, 10(2): 108-123.

Dishion, Thomas J., Joan McCord, and François Poulin. (1999). When interventions harm: Peer groups and harmful behavior. *American Psychologist*, 54(9): 755–764.

Dobson, Kenneth S., and Kate E. Hamilton. (2002). The stage model for psychotherapy manual development: A valuable tool for promoting evidence-based practice. *Clinical Psychology Science and Practice*, 9(4) :407–409.

Dodge, Kenneth A. (2006). Translational science in action: Hostile attributional style and the development of aggressive behavior problems. *Development and Psychopathology*, 18(3): 791–814.

Doss, Brian D., and David C. Atkins. (2006). Investigating treatment mediators when simple random assignment to a control group is not possible. *Clinical Psychology: Science and Practice*, 13(4): 321–336.

Elliott, Delbert S., and Sharon Mihalic. (2004). Issues in disseminating and replicating effective prevention programs. *Prevention Science*, 5(1): 47–53.

Escobar, Javier I., and William A. Vega. (2000). Commentary: Mental health and immigration AAA's: Where are we and where do we go from here? *The Journal of Nervous and Mental Disease*, 188(11): 736–740.

Fairweather, George W., (Ed).(1980). The Fairweather Lodge: A twenty-five year retrospective. *New Directions for Mental Health Services*, no 7. San Francisco, CA: Jossey-Bass.

Federal Bureau of Investigation. (2007). *Uniform crime reports*. Retrieved September 26, 2008 from http://www.fbi.gov/ucr/ucr.htm.

Fischer, Joel. (1973). Is casework effective? *Social Work*, 18(1): 5–20.

Fisher, Ronald Aylmer. (1935). *The design of experiments*. London: Oliver and Boyd.

Fixsen, Dean L., Sandra F. Naoom, Karen A. Blasé, Robert M. Friedman, and Frances Wallace. (2005). *Implementation research: A synthesis of the literature*. Tampa: University of South Florida, Louis de la Parte Florida Mental Health Institute, The National Implementation Research Network (FMHI Publication #231). Retrieved from http://nirn.fmhi.usf.edu/resources/publications/Monograph/pdf/Monograph_full.pdf.

Flay, Brian R. (1986). Efficacy and effectiveness trials (and other phases of research) in the development of health promotion programs. *Preventive Medicine, 15*(5): 451–474.

Fonagy, Peter. (1999). Achieving evidence-based psychotherapy practice: A psychodynamic perspective on the general acceptance of treatment manuals. *Clinical Psychology: Science and Practice, 6*(4): 442–444.

Foxhall, Kathryn. (2000). Research for the real world. *Monitor on Psychology, 31*(7): 28–36.

Fraser, Mark W. (1994). Scholarship and research in social work: Emerging challenges. *Journal of Social Work Education, 30*(2): 252–266.

Fraser, Mark W. (1996a). Aggressive behavior in childhood and early adolescence: An ecological-developmental perspective on youth violence. *Social Work, 41*(4): 347–361.

Fraser, Mark W. (1996b). Cognitive problem-solving and aggressive behavior among children. *Families in Society, 77*(1): 19–32.

Fraser, Mark W., (Ed.). (2004). *Risk and resilience in childhood: An ecological perspective* (2nd ed.). Washington, DC: NASW Press.

Fraser, Mark W. (2008). Social and character development: The competency support program. Preliminary findings. Paper presented an annual meeting of the Social and Character Development Research Group. U.S. Department of Education, Institute of Education Sciences, Washington, DC.

Fraser, Mark W., and David A. Haapala. (1987–1988). Home-based family therapy: A quantitative-qualitative assessment. *The Journal of Applied Social Sciences, 12*(1): 1–23.

Fraser, Mark W., Steven H. Day, Maeda J. Galinksy, Vanessa G. Hodges, and Paul R. Smokowski. (2004). Conduct problems and peer rejection in childhood: A randomized trial of the Making Choices and Strong Families programs. *Research on Social Work Practice, 14*(5): 313–324.

Fraser, Mark W., Maeda J. Galinsky, Paul R. Smokowski, Steven H. Day, Mary A. Terzian, Roderick A. Rose, et al. (2005). Social information-processing skills training to promote social competence and prevent aggressive behavior in third grade. *Journal of Consulting and Clinical Psychology, 73*(6): 1045–1055.

Fraser, Mark W., Jung-Sook Lee, Lawrence L. Kupper, Roderick A. Rose, Paul R. Smokowski, Maeda J. Galinsky, et al. (2007, January 21). Social information-processing skills training to prevent aggressive behavior in the third grade: 6-month follow-up findings from a study of the *Making Choices* program. Paper presented at the 11th Annual Conference of the Society for Social Work and Research, San Francisco, CA.

Fraser, Mark W., James K. Nash, Maeda J. Galinsky, and Kathleen E. Darwin. (2000). *Making choices: Social problem-solving skills for children.* Washington, DC: NASW Press.

Fraser, Mark W., Mary J. Taylor, Robert Jackson, and Jamal O'Jack. (1991). Social work and science: Many ways of knowing? *Social Work Research and Abstracts, 27*(4): 5–15.

Fulbright-Anderson, Karen, Anne C. Kubisch, and James P. Connell, (Eds.). (1998). *New approaches to evaluating community initiatives: Theory, measurement, and analysis.* Washington, DC: Aspen Institute.

Galinsky, Maeda J., Joanne E. Turnbull, Diane E. Meglin, and Margaret E. Wilner. (1993). Confronting the reality of collaborative practice research: Issues of practice, design, measurement, and team development. *Social Work, 38*(4): 440–449.

Galinsky, Maeda J., Mary A. Terzian, and Mark W. Fraser. (2006). The art of group work practice using manualized curricula. *Social Work Practice with Groups, 29*(1): 11–26.

Gamoran, Adam, (Ed.). (2007). *Standards-based reform and the poverty gap: Lessons for "No Child Left Behind."* Washington, DC: Brookings Institution Press.

Garfield, Sol L. (1996). Some problems associated with "validated" forms of psychotherapy. *Clinical Psychology: Science and Practice, 3*(3): 218–229.

Gawande, Atul. (2007, December 10). Annals of medicine: The checklist. *New Yorker 83*(39):86-95.

Gershoff, Elizabeth T., J. Lawrence Aber, C. Cybele Raver, and Mary Clare Lennon. (2007). Income is not enough: Incorporating material hardship into models of income associations with parenting and child development. *Child Development, 78*(1): 70–95.

Gifford-Smith, Mary E., Kenneth A. Dodge, Thomas J. Dishion, and Joan McCord. (2005). Peer influence in children and adolescents: Crossing the bridge from developmental to intervention science. *Journal of Abnormal Child Psychology, 33*(3): 255–265.

Glasgow, Russell E., Edward Lichtenstein, and Alfred C. Marcus. (2003). Why don't we see more translation of health promotion research to practice? Rethinking the efficacy-to-effectiveness transition. *American Journal of Public Health, 93*(8): 1261–1267.

Glasgow, Russell E., Thomas M. Vogt, and Shawn M. Boles. (1999). Evaluating the public health impact of health promotion interventions: The RE-AIM framework. *American Journal of Public Health, 89*(2): 1322–1327.

Glisson, Charles, John Landsverk, Sonja Schoenwald, Kelly Kelleher, Kimberly Eaton Hoagwood, et al. (2008a). Assessing the organizational social context (OSC) of mental health services: Implications for research and practice. *Administration and Policy in Mental Health and Mental Health Services Research, 35*(1–2): 98–113.

Glisson, Charles, John Landsverk, Sonja Schoenwald, Kelly Kelleher, Kimberly Eaton Hoagwood, et al. (2008b). Therapist turnover and new program sustainability in mental health clinics as a function of organizational culture, climate, and service structure. *Administration and Policy in Mental Health and Mental Health Services Research, 35*(1–2): 124–133.

Glueck, Sheldon, and Eleanor Glueck. (1950). *Unraveling juvenile delinquency.* Cambridge, MA: Harvard University Press.

Greenberg, Mark T. (2004). Current and future challenges in school-based prevention: The researcher perspective. *Prevention Science, 5*(1): 5–13.

Greenwald, Peter, and Joseph W. Cullen, (1985). The new emphasis in cancer control. *Journal of the National Cancer Institute, 74*(3): 543–551.

Guillemin, Frances, Claire Bombardier, and Dorcas Beaton. (1993). Cross-cultural adaptation of health-related quality of life measures: Literature review and proposed guidelines. *Journal of Clinical Epidemiology, 46*(12): 1417–1432.

Guo, Shenyang, and Mark W. Fraser. (In press). *Propensity score analysis: Statistical methods and applications.* Thousand Oaks, CA: Sage.

Halliday-Boykins, Colleen A., and Scott W. Henggeler. (2001). Multisystemic therapy: Theory, research, and practice. In (Elaine Walton, Patricia Sandau-Beckler, and Mark Mannes, (Eds.), *Balancing family-centered services and child well-being* (pp. 320–335). New York: Columbia University Press.

Harris, and Associates. (1997). *School Success Profile.* (Study number 628173). New York: Author.

Harrison, Diane F., Walter W. Hudson, and Bruce A. Thyer. (1992). On a critical analysis of empirical clinical practice: A response to Witkin's revised views. *Social Work, 37*(5): 461–464.

Havelock, Ronald G. (1969). *Planning for innovation: A comparative study of the literature on the dissemination and utilization of scientific knowledge.* Ann Arbor: Center for Research on Utilization of Scientific Knowledge, University of Michigan.

Havelock, Ronald G. (1995). *The change agent's guide* (2nd ed.). Englewood Cliffs, NJ: Educational Technology Publications.

Hawkins, J. David. (2006). Science, social work, prevention: Finding the intersections. *Social Work Research, 30*(3): 137–152.

Haynes, R. Brian, P. J. Devereaux, and Gordan H. Guyatt. (2002, March/April). Clinical expertise in the era of evidence-based medicine and patient choice. *ACP Journal Club, 136*: A11–A14.

Heimberg, Richard G., and Robert E. Becker. (2002). *Cognitive-behavioral group therapy for social phobia.* New York: Guilford Press.

Henderson, Joanna L., Sherri MacKay, and Michele Peterson-Badali. (2006). Closing the research-practice gap: Factors affecting adoption and implementation of a children's mental health program. *Journal of Clinical Child and Adolescent Psychology, 35*(1): 2–12.

Henggeler, Scott W., and Charles M. Borduin. (1992). *Multisystemic therapy adherence scales*. Charleston: Medical University of South Carolina, Department of Psychiatry and Behavioral Science.

Howard, Matthew O., and Jeffery M. Jenson. (1999). Clinical practice guidelines: Should social work develop them? *Research on Social Work Practice, 9*(3): 283–301.

Hudson, Walter W. (1978). Research training in professional social work education. *Social Service Review, 52*(1): 116–121.

Hudson, Walter W. (1982). Scientific imperatives in social work research and practice. *Social Service Review, 56*(2): 246–258.

Institute for the Advancement of Social Work Research. (2007). *Partnerships to integrate evidence-based mental health practices into social work education and research*. Retrieved September 26, 2008 from http://www.charityadvantge. com/iaswr/EvidenceBasedPracticeFinal.pdf.

Institute of Medicine. (2001). *Crossing the quality chasm: A new health care system for the 21st century*. Washington, DC: National Academy Press.

Jenson, Jeffrey M., and Mark W. Fraser (Eds.). (2006). *Social policy for children and families: A risk and resilience perspective*. Thousand Oaks, CA: Sage.

Jilcott, Stephanie, Alice Ammerman, Janice Sommers, and Russell E. Glasgow. (2007). Applying the RE-AIM framework to assess the public health impact of policy change. *Annals of Behavioral Medicine, 34*(2): 105–114.

Kazdin, Alan E. (2001). Progression of therapy research and clinical application of treatment require better understanding of the change process. *Clinical Psychology: Science and Practice, 8*(2): 143–151.

Kendall, Philip C. (1998). Directing misperceptions: Researching the issues facing manual-based treatments. *Clinical Psychology: Science and Practice, 5*(3): 396–399.

Kessler, Ronald C., Peter J. Pecora, Jay Williams, Eva Hiripi, Kirk O'Brien, Diana English, et al. (2008). Effects of enhanced foster care on the long-term physical and mental health of foster care alumni. *Archives of General Psychiatry, 65*(6): 625–633.

Last, John M. (1988). *A dictionary of epidemiology*. New York: Oxford University Press.

Lau, Anna S. (2006). Making the case for selective and directed cultural adaptations of evidence-based treatments: Examples from parent training. *Clinical Psychology: Science and Practice, 13*(4): 295–310.

Lemerise, Elizabeth A., and William F. Arsenio. (2000). An integrated model of emotion processes and cognition in social information processing. *Child Development, 71*(1): 107–118.

Littell, Julia H. (2005) Lessons from a systematic review of effects of multisystemic therapy. *Children and Youth Services Review, 27*(4): 445-463.

Luborsky, Lester. (1999). The researcher's own therapy allegiances: A "wild card"' in comparisons of treatment efficacy. *Clinical Psychology Science and Practice, 6*(1): 95–106.

Luborsky, Lester, and Robert J. DeRubeis. (1984). The use of psychotherapy treatment manuals: A small revolution in psychotherapy research style. *Clinical Psychology Review, 4* (1): 5–14.

Luborsky, Lester, Brian Singer, and L. Luborsky. (1975). Comparative studies of psychotherapies: Is it true that "everybody has won and all must have prizes"? *Archives of General Psychiatry, 32*(8): 995–1008.

Maluccio, John A., and Rafael Flores. (2004, July). *Impact evaluation of a conditional cash transfer program: The Nicaraguan Red De Proteccion Social.* Washington, DC: International Food Policy Research Institute (FCND Discussion Paper No. 184). Retrieved from http://www.ifpri.org/divs/fcnd/dp/papers/fcndp184.pdf.

Marin, Gerardo, Fabio Sabogal, Barbara Vanoss Marin, Regina Otero-Sabogal, and Eliseo J. Perez-Stable. (1987). Development of a short acculturation scale for Hispanics. *Hispanic Journal of Behavioral Sciences, 9*(2): 183–205.

Marmot, Michael. (2005). Social determinants of health inequalities. *Lancet, 365*(9464): 1099–1104.

Martinez, Charles R., Jr., and J. Mark Eddy. (2005). Effects of culturally adapted parent management training on Latino youth behavioral health outcomes. *Journal of Consulting and Clinical Psychology, 73*(4): 841–851.

McCord, Joan. (1992). The Cambridge–Somerville Study: A pioneering longitudinal-experimental study of delinquency prevention. In (Joan McCord, and Richard E. Tremblay, (Eds.), *Preventing antisocial behavior: Interventions from birth through adolescence* (pp. 196–206). New York: Guilford Press.

McDavid, James C., and Laura R. L. Hawthorn. (2006). *Program evaluation and performance measurement: An introduction to practice.* Thousand Oaks, CA: Sage.

Meyer, Henry J., Edgar F. Borgatta, and Wyatt C. Jones. (1965). *Girls at vocational high: An experiment in social work intervention.* New York: Russell Sage Foundation.

Midgley, Gerald. (2006). Systemic intervention in public health. *American Journal of Public Health, 96*(3): 466–472.

Miller, William R., and Stephen Rollnick. (2002). *Motivational interviewing: Preparing people to change.* New York: Guilford Press.

Mowbray, Carol T., Mark C. Holter, Gregory B. Teague, and Deborah Bybee. (2003). Fidelity criteria: Development, measurement, and validation. *American Journal of Evaluation, 24*(3): 315–340.

Najavits, Lisa M., Roger D. Weiss, Sarah Shaw, and Amy Dierberger. (2000). Psychotherapists' views of treatment manuals. *Professional Psychology: Research and Practice, 31*(4): 404–408.

Nash, James K. (2002). Neighborhood effects on sense of school coherence and educational behavior in students at risk of school failure. *Children and Schools, 24*(2): 73–89.

Nash, James K., Mark W. Fraser, Maeda J. Galinsky, and Lawrence L. Kupper. (2003). Early development and pilot testing of a problem-solving skills-training program for children. *Research on Social Work Practice, 13*(4): 432–450.

National Association of Social Workers. (2007). *Code of ethics-Preamble.* Retrieved September 26, 2008 from http://www.socialworkers.org/pubs/code/code.asp.

National Institute of Mental Health. (2007a). *Suicide in the U.S.: Statistics and prevention.* Retrieved September 28, 2008 from http://www.nimh.nih.gov/health/publications/suicide-in-the-us-statistics-and-prevention.shtml.

National Institute of Mental Health. (2007b). *The numbers count: Mental disorders in America.* Retrieved September 26, 2008 from http://www.nimh.nih.gov/health/publications/the-numbers-count-mental-disorders-in-america.shtml#Intro.

National Institutes of Health. (2006, October). *Health Disparities Fact Sheet.* Retrieved July 3, 2008 from: http://www.nih.gov/about/researchresultsforthepublic/HealthDisparities.pdf.

North, Michael S., Alissa A. Gleacher, Marleen Radigan, Lindsay Greene, Jessica Mass Levitt, Janet Chassman, et al. (2008). The Evidence-Based Treatment Dissemination Center: Bridging the research-practice gap in New York State. *Report on Emotional and Behavioral Disorders in Youth, 8*(1): 9–16.

Office of Mental Health. (2008). *Clinical training for childhood depression and trauma bringing evidence based treatment to children and adolescents.* New York: State Office of Mental Health. Retrieved July 14, 2008from http://www.omh.state.ny.us/omhweb/resources/clinical_training/presentation.html.

Office of Science Policy. (2005, November 14–15). *Considering usual medical care in clinical trial design: Scientific and ethical issues.* Conference organized by the National Institutes of Health Program on Clinical Research Policy Analysis and Coordination. Washington, DC.

Okwuje, Ifie, and Nicholas Johnson. (2006). A rising number of state earned income tax credits are helping working families escape poverty. Washington, DC: Center on Budget and Policy Priorities. Retrieved July 16, 2008 from http://www.cbpp.org/10-12-06sfp.htm.

Olds, David L., Harriet Kitzman, Carole Hanks, Robert Cole, Elizabeth Anson, Kimberley Sidora-Arcoleo, et al. (2007). Effects of nurse home visiting on maternal and child functioning: Age-9 follow-up of a randomized trial. *Pediatrics, 120*(4): e832–e845.

Onken, Lisa S., Jack D. Blaine, and Robert J. Battjes. (1997). Behavioral therapy research: A conceptualization of a process. In Scott W. Henggeler, and

Alberto B. Santos, (Eds.), *Innovative approaches for difficult to treat populations* (pp. 477–485). Washington, DC: American Psychiatric Press.

Pecora, Peter J., Ronald C. Kessler, Jay Williams, A.C. Downs, Diana English, Diana, James White, and Kirk O'Brien. (Forthcoming). *What works in foster care?* Oxford: Oxford University Press.

Petticrew, Mark, and H. Roberts. (2003). Evidence, hierarchies, and typologies: Horses for courses. *Journal of Epidemiology and Community Health, 57*(7): 527–529.

Porter, Andrew C., and Morgan S. Polikoff. (2007). NCLB: State interpretations, early effects, and suggestions for reauthorization. *Social Policy Report, 21*(4): 3–14. Retreived from http://www.srcd.org/documents/publications/spr/21-4_no_child_ left_behind.pdf.

Powers, Edwin, Helen Witmer, and Gordon Allport. (1951). *An experiment in the prevention of delinquency: The Cambridge-Somerville Youth Study.* New York: Columbia University Press.

Prochaska, James O., Kerry E. Evers, Janice M. Prochaska, Deborah Van Marter, and Janet L. Johnson. (2007). Efficacy and effectiveness trials: Examples from smoking cessation and bullying prevention. *Journal of Health Psychology, 12*(1): 170–178.

Proctor, Enola K., and Aaron Rosen. (2003). The structure and function of social work practice guidelines. In Aaron Rosen, and Enola K. Proctor (Eds.), *Developing practice guidelines for social work intervention: Issues, methods, and research agenda* (pp. 108–127). New York: Columbia University Press.

Pronovost, Peter, Dale Needham, Sean Berenholtz, David Sinopoli, Haitao Chu, Sara Cosgrove, et al: (2006). An intervention to decrease catheter-related bloodstream infections in the ICU. *New England Journal of Medicine, 355*(26): 2725–2732.

RAND Corporation. (2007). *Promising practices network.* Retrieved from http:// www.promisingpractices.net.

RAND Corporation. (2008). SF-36: 36-item short form survey. Retrieved rom http://www.rand.org/health/surveys_tools/mos/mos_core_36item.html.

Richman, Jack M., and Gary L. Bowen. (1997). School failure: An ecological-interactional-developmental perceptive. In Mark W. Fraser (Ed.), *Risk and resiliency in childhood: An ecological perspective* (pp. 95–116). Washington, DC: NASW Press.

Richman, Jack M., Gary L. Bowen, and Michael E. Woolley. (2004). School failure: An ecological-interactional-developmental perceptive. In Mark W. Fraser (Ed.), *Risk and resiliency in childhood: An ecological perspective* (2nd ed., pp. 133–160). Washington, DC: NASW Press.

Richman, Jack M., Lawrence B. Rosenfeld, and Gary L. Bowen. (1998). Social support for adolescents at risk of school failure. *Social Work, 43*(4): 309–323.

Ringwalt, Christopher L., Susan T. Ennett, Amy A. Vincus, Judy Thorne, Louise Ann Rohrbach, and Ashley Simons-Rudolph. (2002). The prevalence of effective substance use prevention curricula in U.S. middle schools. *Prevention Science, 3*(4): 257–265.

Rivera, Daniel E., Michael D. Pew, and Linda M. Collins. (2007). Using engineering control principles to inform the design of adaptive interventions: A conceptual introduction. *Drug and Alcohol Dependence, 88S*: S31–S40.

Rivera, Juan A., Daniela Sotres-Álvarez, Jean-Pierre Habicht, Teresa Shamah, and Salvador Billapando. (2004). Impact of the Mexican program for education, health, and nutrition (Progresa) on rates of growth and anemia in infants and young children: A randomized effectiveness study. *Journal of the American Medical Association, 291*(21): 2563–2570.

Rogers, Everett. M. (1995). *Diffusion of innovations* (4th ed.). New York: Free Press.

Rossi, Peter H., Mark W. Lipsey, and Howard E. Freeman. (2003). *Evaluation: A systematic approach* (7th ed.). Thousand Oaks, CA: Sage.

Rowland, Melisa D., Colleen A. Halliday-Boykins, Scott W. Henggeler, Phillippe B. Cunningham, Terry G. Lee, Markus J. P. Kruesi, and Steven B. Shapiro. (2005). A randomized trial of multisystemic therapy with Hawaii's Felix Class youths. *Journal of Emotional and Behavioral Disorders, 13*(1): 13-23.

Rothman, Jack, and Edwin J. Thomas, (Eds.). (1994). *Intervention research: Design and development for human services*. New York: Haworth Press.

Rounsaville, Bruce J., Kathleen M. Carroll, and Lisa S. Onken. (2001). A stage model of behavioral therapies research: Getting started and moving on from stage I. *Clinical Psychology Science and Practice, 8*(2): 133–142.

Sackett David L., William M. C. Rosenberg, J. A. Muir Gray, R. Brian Haynes, and W. Scott Richardson. (1996). Evidence based medicine: what it is and what it isn't: It's about integrating individual clinical expertise and the best external evidence. *British Medical Journal, 312*(7023): 71–72.

Saleebey, Dennis. (2005). *The strengths perspective in social work practice* (4th ed.). New York: Allyn & Bacon.

Schoenwald, Sonja K., Ashli J. Sheidow, and Elizabeth J. Letourneau. (2004). Toward effective quality assurance in evidence-based practice: Links between expert consultation, therapist fidelity, and child outcomes. *Journal of Clinical Child and Adolescent Psychology, 33*(1): 94–104.

Schreiner, Mark, Michael Sherraden, Margaret Clancy, Lissa Johnson, Jamie Curley, Min Zhan, *et al.* (2005). Assets and the poor: Evidence from individual development accounts. In Michael Sherraden (Ed.), *Inclusion in the American dream: Assets, poverty, and public policy* (185–215). New York: Oxford University Press.

Schwalbe, Craig S., Mark W. Fraser, and Steven H. Day. (2007). Predictive validity of the Joint Risk Matrix with juvenile offenders: A focus on gender and race/ethnicity. *Criminal Justice and Behavior*, 34(3):348–361.

Shadish, William R., Thomas D. Cook, and Donald T. Campbell. (2002). *Experimental and quasi-experimental designs for generalized causal inference.* New York: Houghton Mifflin.

Shaya, Fadia T., and Anna Gu. (2006). Deriving effectiveness information for decision making. *Expert Reviews of Pharmoeconomics and Outcomes Research*, 6(1): 5–7.

Smokowski, Paul R., Mark W. Fraser, Steven H. Day, Maeda J. Galinksy, and Martica L. Bacallao. (2004). School-based skills training to prevent aggressive behavior and peer rejection in childhood: Evaluating the *Making Choices* program. *Journal of Primary Prevention*, 25(2): 233–251.

Snyder, James, John Reid, Mike Stoolmiller, George Howe, Hendricks Brown, Getachew Dagne, and Wendi Cross. (2006). The role of behavior observation in measurement systems for randomized prevention trials. *Prevention Science*, 7(1): 43–56.

Society for Prevention Research, Standards of Evidence Committee. (2004). *Standards of evidence: Criteria for efficacy, effectiveness and dissemination.* Society for Prevention Research. Retrieved from http://www.preventionresearch. org/StandardsofEvidencebook.pdf.

Society for Prevention Research, Standards of Evidence Committee. (2007). *Standards of evidence: Criteria for efficacy, effectiveness, and dissemination.* Retrieved from http://www.preventionresearch.org/StandardsofEvidencebook.pdf.

Substance Abuse and Mental Health Services Administration. (2007). *Model programs: Effective substance abuse and mental health programs for every community.* Retrieved September 26, 2008 from http://www.modelprograms. samhsa.gov

Sundell, Knut, Kjell Hansson, Cecilia Andrée Löfholm, Tina Olsson, Lars-Henry Custle, and Christina Kadesjö (2008). The transportability of multisystemic therapy to Sweden: Short-term results from a randomize trial of conduct-disordered youths. *Journal of Family Psychology*, 22(3): 550-560.

Sussman Steve, Thomas W. Valente, Louise A. Rohrbach, Silvana Skara, and Mary Ann Pentz. (2006). Translation in the health professions: Converting science into action. *Evaluation and the Health Professions*, 29(1): 7–32.

Timmons-Mitchell, Jane, Monica B. Bender, Maureen A. Kishna, and Clare C. Mitchell. (2006). An independent effectiveness trial of multisystemic therapy with juvenile justice youth. *Journal of Clinical Child and Adolescent Psychology*, 35(2): 227-236.

Tripodi, Tony, and Irwin Epstein. (1980). *Research techniques for clinical social workers.* New York: Columbia University Press.

Tripodi, Tony, Phillip A. Fellin, and Irwin Epstein. (1978). *Differential social program evaluation*. Itasca, IL: F. E. Peacock.

Trochim, William, M. K. (2005). *Research methods: The concise knowledge base*. Cincinnati, OH: Atomic Dog.

U.S. Department of Education. (2007). *What works clearinghouse*. Retrieved from http://www.whatworks.ed.gov.

U.S. Department of Health and Human Services. (2008). Trends in foster care and adoption. Administration for Children and Families, Children's Bureau. Retrieved from http://www.acf.hhs.gov/programs/cb/stats_research/afcars/trends.htm.

van Widenfelt, Brigit M., Phillip D.A. Treffers, Edwin de Beurs, Bart M. Siebelink, and Els Koudijs. (2005). Translation and cross-cultural adaptation of assessment instruments in psychological research with children and families. *Clinical Child and Family Psychological Review*, 8(2): 135–146.

Wagner, Eric F., Cynthia C. Swenson, and Scott W. Henggeler. (2000). Practical and methodological challenges in validating community-based interventions. *Children's Services: Social Policy, Research, and Practice*, 3(4): 211–231.

Weisz, John R., Amanda L. Jensen, and Bruce D. McLeod. (2005). Milestones and methods in the development and dissemination of child and adolescent psychotherapies: Review, commentary, and a new deployment-focused model. In Euthymia D. Hibbs, and Peter S. Jensen, (Eds.), *Psychosocial treatments for child and adolescent disorders: Empirically based strategies for clinical practice* (2nd ed., pp. 9–39). Washington, DC: American Psychological Association.

Wilson, G. Terence. (1996). Manual-based treatments: The clinical application of research findings. *Behaviour Research and Therapy*, 34(4): 295–314.

Witkin, Stanley L. (1991). Empirical clinical practice: A critical analysis. *Social Work*, 36(2) 158–163.

Wolpe, Joseph. (1969). *The practice of behavior therapy*. New York: Pergamon Press.

Index

The following elements in text are indicated by italic abbreviations: *f*, figure; *t*, table; *tb*, text box.

39615018R00128

Made in the USA
Middletown, DE
20 January 2017